ALL EARS

ALL EARS

MICHAEL HOLDEN

Illustrated by

ANDY WATT

ALMA BOOKS

ALMA BOOKS LTD
London House
243–253 Lower Mortlake Road
Richmond
Surrey TW9 2LL
United Kingdom
www.almabooks.com

Printed in Jordan by the National Press

ISBN-13 (HARDBACK): 978-1-84688-038-4
ISBN-10 (HARDBACK): 1-84688-038-6

For Mum & Dad

INTRODUCTION

There's nothing dignified about listening to other people's conversations, but modern life has made it unavoidable. It wasn't something that I set out to do, but it wasn't till I did that I realized just how much there was to hear. If you live in a city, and especially if you don't drive a car, then the conversations of strangers are everywhere. They're like static. There is no need to skulk about to collect them: you just need to tune yourself in. And there's nothing shameful about it either. In the contemporary climate of global-surveillance hysteria, the action of simply noting down what is said around you because you like the sound of it is comparatively benign. If people think they aren't being listened to on some level in the twenty-first century, then they're just not paying enough attention.

All Ears was born partly from a desire to highlight how unusual and unscriptable everyday conversation can be, and partly because I wished people would just shut up. Like most of us I have made conversational currency of things I've heard other people say. When we meet, such disclosures are often the prelude to the more routine components of conversation. What we are perhaps less conscious of is that the stuff we stumble across and relate by chance can be a lot more interesting than the things we set out to try and say.

The idea to start collating this material came from a radio presenter, who suggested – after an exchange of overheard anecdotes – that I wear a wire with the intention of recording broadcast-quality sound bites to play back on his show. This quickly proved unfeasible. Given the technology of the time, it would have required a proximity to the subject that would risk detection, and the kind of placid acoustic environments seldom found in everyday existence. Nevertheless, I kept rough written records of some of the things I heard, resurrecting and embellishing them verbally when the opportunity arose.

Three years after the abandoned radio scheme, a newly launched magazine, *Good for Nothing*, offered me a column without specifying what the content would be. The caveat for this unlikely moment of editorial freedom was that it would be unpaid. 'Earwigging' – as it was then known – began appearing monthly in the winter of 2003. At this time I had a job that required a total of four hours of peak-time commuting each day. Where previously I had been striving to block out ambient sound, I set aside my headphones and listened in. My reluctant proximity to hundreds of other miserable travellers was rendered marginally more bearable by detailing it in print. And the chatter was always there, you didn't have to go out of your way to find it.

After three months events took an altogether more serious complexion when the *Guardian* expressed an interest in carrying the column. The fact that they were willing to pay for it too overrode the loyalties I felt to its initial publisher, so I moved on. What was worrying was that the new 'All Ears' column would be weekly. Whilst you'd have to be wilfully reclusive not to overhear something halfway interesting on a monthly basis, doing it every week would be a different matter. My fear was that I would be forced by the terms of my contract into making conversations up. Instead, the more I listened, the more I heard. You have no idea what you're tuning out until you let it in.

In much the same way as governments justify their eavesdropping as a "wartime measure" conducted for the good of democracy, I embarked on a covert campaign of my own in pursuit of the weekly deadline. Not that you have to try too hard. Where careless talk once cost lives, these days life seems to consist of little else. That said, I could never have done it without the mobile phone.

Mobiles have rendered what was once private horribly public. The discretion that came with making a call at home, at work or in a phone box evaporated in the 1990s. Medical matters, marital strife, threats, disclosures, promises and a tidal wave of bewitching trivia were all there for the taking. As well as destroying what was left of public discretion, the mobile also provided a valuable alibi for the practising eavesdropper. Lingering about aimlessly is still viewed with some suspicion and can cause people to clam up, but if you clamp a dead mobile to your ear and act like you're listening, then nobody pays you any heed.

The other benefit of the technology is that it offers another means to record what you've heard. I soon discovered that even if you sit next to someone with a pen and paper and start writing, it never occurs to them that you might be writing about them. But there are always situations where writing just isn't possible. When this happens, I phone myself up and leave a message describing what I've heard.

Within weeks of the *Guardian* column appearing people began responding to it, often prefacing their remarks with "You'd better not be writing any of this down". But the burning issue from most of the people I met was and continues to be whether the conversations are made up. My response to this is a resounding "no", though I never feel that people really believe me. I knew at the outset that once I started resorting to fiction, then the gig was effectively up. In fact the whole point of the exercise – as far as it can be said to have one – is to demonstrate the abiding principle that truth is always stranger than fiction. My stock response to enquiries about the veracity of the stories is that if I could make up dialogue like that I would be working in Hollywood rather than mooching around launderettes in East London hoping someone will say something. There are embellishments and compromises in the name of editorial expediency, but the real business of it, the quotes and the language that people are moved to question, is always as true as my methods allow.

This is abundantly clear in the 'Clock on a Stick' story (page 59). If I sat at a computer for the rest of my life, I doubt I would be able to imagine anything quite so vivid and unlikely as what those men said at a pedestrian crossing on a summer's afternoon. The only problem I ever faced in acquiring anecdotes was when I spent long periods of time working from home. You get the odd one in the closed circuit of your local haunts, but the big game dwells further afield, and you must take steps to hunt it down.

Some places are more fruitful than others and, from a winning combination of duration and proximity, public transport consistently comes out on top. The agonizing pace of the average bus journey is such that someone invariably says something in person or over the phone to someone else, whether it's of any interest or in a language you speak is another matter entirely. Railways, the source of the original "I'm on the train" mobile-phone cliché, remain a happy hunting ground. Airport departure lounges are the eavesdropper's equivalent of a January sale. Galleries, though arguably offering a less varied range of subject, are good because you are free to stand very close to other people without appearing odd – though some of the better conversations have come from the staff of public buildings, rather than the public themselves. Restaurants and cafés are full of people talking far too loudly. Indeed, the more people are paying to be somewhere, the louder they seem to be.

Last in the hit parade of consistently chat-ridden locales is the public house. If you know of one nearby that boasts the kind of clientele who think nothing of striking up conversation with complete strangers or simply argue loudly among themselves, then so much the better.

So while the broad patterns of existence afford us access to a whole universe of unsolicited detail, to get the best of it – and certainly to get a good story every week – you might need to amend your behaviour within it. Ordinarily I would instinctively seek out a table or seat in any venue as far away as possible from anyone else; now I sit near the noisiest people I can find. I have missed my stop on buses and stretched out drinks far beyond their intended lifespan; I have had to tell people I was genuinely conversing with to shut up for a minute, and followed strangers on mobiles down streets that led nowhere I meant to go.

Doing something for a living ought to stop you from wondering why you're bothering to do it, but in fact the reverse is true. The more I listened, the more I found myself wondering what it was that I was hoping to hear. I think the reasons I got so wrapped up in it – and it has become a kind of conditioned reflex that functions beyond the requirements of publishing – are twofold. Firstly, it's exciting. It adds a layer of espionage to the everyday and, like fishing, after periods where nothing happens the smallest bite becomes intoxicating. Secondly, I still believe that there are things in the spontaneous speech of strangers that tell us something about ourselves that the media – no matter how determined it might seem in its quest to beguile us with "reality" – does not deliver. Exactly *what* it's saying I have no idea, but I'm certain that it's there.

The moment which I dread and crave in equal measure, when the whole business folds in on itself in some ghastly postmodern collapse, is when I overhear someone talking about something they have read about me overhearing. Then, maybe, it will be time to stop, and I can imagine that we have instigated a thriving culture of benign surveillance where we listen more carefully to each other, look less intently to the media for entertainment and inspiration, consider more thoroughly the possibilities of what we are already saying, and say it nonetheless.

– Michael Holden, August 2007

ALL EARS

Dog Death

Marooned in one of those unfeasibly long yet remarkably calm queues that are now the defining characteristic of air travel, time passed more swiftly thanks to a couple who were reminiscing over previous holiday disasters.

Man (in his mid-thirties, a bit careworn and visibly distressed by the memories he was resurrecting) "They never even told us the dog was sick."

Woman (aghast) "No!"

Man "They'd said it was old is all, and it needed some medicine. But when we got there it was obviously dying – it smelt like death, dog death. They should have put it down years ago, but couldn't bring themselves to do it. It was asthmatic, rheumatic and had cysts that you had to rub cream into. It breathed like it had a punctured lung, and every breath sounded like its last."

Woman "That's so wrong."

Man "Completely unnecessary. My first instinct was to put it out of its misery, and just say it had died while we were there, but there was a big note on the fridge."

Woman "Saying 'Don't Kill the Dog!'?"

Man "No, it was more like a list, a few pages of A4 about what to do with all these medicines, which vet to call if it took a turn for the worse. Very thorough. The implication, I felt, was that they were saying, "We'll know if you killed it.""

Woman "So what did you do?"

Man "Looked after it. Made it as comfortable as possible. Obviously it did detract from the beauty of the location somewhat, but I grew to like it. It was a good holiday in some ways."

Woman "How was that?"

Man "Well it put me more in touch with my own mortality."

Woman "You don't get that in Ibiza."

Man "Oh, I dunno."

Poirot

On the occasion of the recent Champions League Final, having been elbowed out of my local pub, I found myself viewing the event on a wide-screen projector in the basement of what was in effect a modernized version of a 1980s "wine bar". Unaccustomed to hosting such occasions, the venue had rigged up some low-rent form of satellite feed, which meant that the coverage was routinely interrupted by large pixelated blocks of digital interference, whining feedback and the occasional out-right blackout. Needless to say this didn't go down well with the more partisan members of the audience, in particular a group of three suited office workers whose annoyance turned to anger as the game went on.

Man 1 (speaking on behalf of the whole bar) "This is fuckin' outrageous. Sort it out."

Barman (in a French accent) "There's nothing I can do. It's not our problem."

Man 2 (as the picture froze again into a mass of coloured cubes) "It's like watching *Predator*!"

Man 1 "It's like fucking Ceefax!"

Man 3 (trying to calm things down) "Well it is raining. Maybe that's the problem."

Man 1 "It's got nothing to do with the rain, it's these pricks in 'ere, they dunno what they're doing."

Man 3 (to the barman) "Come on mate, there must be something you can do?"

Barman "I'm telling you, it's not my problem, that's just the way it is."

It was then that the screen went off completely, only for coverage to resume moments later after a goal had been scored.

Man 1 (assembling his belongings and gesturing to his friends) "This is out of order, let's get out of here."

Man 3 "You sure there's nothing you can do?"

The barman shook his head.

Man 1 "I'm off, and I won't be coming back here for the World Cup, I can promise you that, mate."

Barman (taking his life in his hands) "No? Well you won't be winning that either."

Man 2 (in an inspired retort) "Fuck off, Poirot!"

With that they left, and the game somehow ceased to matter.

Bank

It was one of those occasions in a bank queue when things are moving so slowly that time appears to have no meaning at all. There were two tellers working, both engaged in transactions of such a protracted nature that one could only speculate as to what aspects of contemporary banking could be so agonizing.

Teller (having gazed at a screen for what seemed like fifteen minutes) "There's no transfer direct from your Delta account."

Man "No?"

Teller (having tapped at her keyboard for a bit) "No."

The man then began to fill up the chute in the counter with an array of dog-eared bank books and weird-looking bags that bought an audible sigh from the queue. I looked down at the bench in front of me and saw that someone had carved "WHY ARE THINGS SO SLOW IN HERE?" into the wood with a ballpoint. The other teller was just staring at the other customer being served as though they were having a competition.

Man "Have you got any of them cardboard tubes?"

Teller "Tubes?"

Man "For putting coins together."

Teller "We only have the bags."

Man "Bags?"

Teller (holding one up to show him what a bag is) "Bags."

Man "I wanted the tubes."

I was just considering what proportion of bank robberies were born out of frustration rather than greed when the second teller's printer rattled into life and produced a form that she handed to her customer.

Teller 2 "Just sign that for me."

The man then began to read what was evidently a detailed but commonplace form in its entirety. Tube man was now struggling to make a pen work. I tried to avoid sinking to my knees and weeping, and resolved to start putting money in a mattress instead.

Kebab

That kebab shops are crucibles of human instability is news to no one. But at 8 p.m. on a weekday evening you'd think you'd be safe. Not a bit of it. No sooner had my shish hit the griddle than an obese man sporting immaculate state-of-the-art hip-hop chic rolled in and announced, "I need to charge my phone," in a booming, mid-Atlantic way. I assumed he was a regular customer – he had the figure for it. But from the look of bafflement on the faces of the staff this was a new one, even for them.

There was a silence, which the man exploited to further his case. "I was talking to a girl," he said, "when my battery ran out." "This is a kebab shop," said the cook. "Charge my phone," said the man.

Man (noticing a phone charger in a wall socket) "C'mon man, give me some power."

Cook (aware that the proximity of the charger undermined his position) "I can't do it my friend, I will lose my job. Ask the manager."

The manager had been at the back of the shop talking on a landline the whole time. He could see exactly what was happening and was in no hurry to get involved. To his credit the man waited a full five minutes for him to hang up.

Man (suddenly sounding reasonable) "I need to charge my phone for a minute."

Manager (surrendering the moral high ground completely) "I can't do that. You need to speak to the owner."

Man "You don't have enough heart in your chest to give me some power?"

There was no response. Then another customer, an early-evening drunk, waved a french fry at the man and announced with a giggle, "You've got a chip on your shoulder!" The man glared at him as though he might, quite literally, consume him for breakfast, and walked out of the shop. Idiots, I thought. You've lost a hell of a customer there.

Cider Women

Taking a seat on a busy train at ten o'clock in the morning, I assumed that the can of White Lightning cider on the table could have nothing to do with the respectable if slightly ragged middle-aged woman sitting next me. However, when she began speaking to her friend in the opposite seat, the fact that they were both members of the early-morning-apple-juice club became abundantly clear.

Woman 1 (slurring from behind cheap sunglasses the size of beer mats) "I wouldn't mind goin' Euro Disney."

Woman 2 (posher but equally pickled) "That's more for kids. I went to Alton Towers. There were things there the like I'd never seen before. Fabulous carousels, extraordinary."

Woman 1 (changing the subject) "Annie last night said she couldn't understand that I'd had a terrible marriage. But I said since I'd been addicted to the old you-know-what, it just makes you oblivious, nothing else matters."

Woman 2 (producing more cider from a discreet stash beneath her seat) "And it's so destructive."

Woman 1 (suddenly angry) "Why haven't I heard from Poppy?"

Woman 2 "Well she's on a retreat, she'll probably come back all reinvigorated."

Woman 1 "Give us your phone." She punched in a number, got up and elbowed her way through the packed carriage. "Colin, it's me. I've lost my phone!" she screamed, before making a conspicuous hash of smoking a cigarette in the toilet. She returned in a pall of smoke, stabbing at the phone with her huge fingers. "I hate texts. I hate 'em."

Woman 2 "Do you think it's hot outside?"

Woman 1 "They said it would be."

Woman 2 "Nearly there!"

As the train approached the station, they leapt up to be the first to leave. I passed them on the platform, where they had sat down immediately for a cigarette.

Woman 1 "Where we going for lunch?"

Woman 2 "Anywhere that has wine."

Landmines

Sharing a table in a modern "canteen-style" restaurant, I found myself clashing elbows with a pair of young men reflecting upon the pressures and excesses of the holiday season.

Man 1 "I got it off me dad of course. Someone said 'bent', and he immediately goes, 'Oh, ask Martin, *he'd* know about that!'"

Man 2 "They don't talk about it then?"

Man 1 "Well, no one ever says anything, but you know – they know. Anyway I feel terrible. God I was pissed last night. Jack Daniels and Stella."

Man 2 (with revulsion) "Stella?"

Man 1 (ashamed) "Stella. But that was nothing. Stevo had a McDonald's! He was all over the place later going, 'Oh I can feel the E numbers coming through my pores!'"

Man 2 (staring into the distance) "Oh, he's such a heartbreaker."

Man 1 "Isn't he just? We were out on the pull and I

ended up talking to some bloke who lobbies for land-mines."

Man 2 "What do you mean?"

Man 1 "You know, he works for the arms industry."

Man 2 (disgusted again) "Oh, he deserves to be strangled!"

Man 1 "He did PR for them as well."

Man 2 (looking forlorn) "How dreadful."

Man 1 "Anyway, it turns out they're not called land-mines any more: they're called close-proximity weapons, or something."

Man 2 "As if that makes a difference! What a job."

Man 1 "I said to him, 'Just don't do it, you know, just stop.'"

Man 2 "What did he do?"

Man 1 "He just laughed and bought more drinks."

With that he ordered another bottle of wine, seeming-ly resigned to the fact that the alcohol and arms industries appeared to be working in tandem against his better nature.

Eastern Promise

You know you're getting older when you go to parties where not only is there food, but people actually sit around eating it. It was at a do like this, where the host had taken the trouble of laying out Japanese snacks, that the following exchange between two men who appeared to be relative strangers rang out across an otherwise silent room.

Man 1 (evidently the more socially enthusiastic of the pair) "Of course, I've been to Japan."

Man 2 (staring at his plate) "Really."

Man 1 "You been?"

Man 2 "I haven't, no."

Man 1 (seizing the chance to act the seasoned traveller) "Well there's this place up north, I forget the name but it's like a big black mountain. Down south the people are in a better mood, mind you. It's like Hawaii or something, but you're in Japan. Anyway you go up north, there's this mountain and then there's a bar – if you can find it – and apparently you can get a beer and they'll wank you off at the same time."

The temperature of the room dropped tangibly and Man 2 froze mid-mouthful as though struck by a bullet.

Man 1 (oblivious) "It's only about a tenner for the whole thing, so I'm told. I've never been."

Man 2 (having crammed enough food into his mouth to absolve himself from fully responding) "Mmmhn…"

Man 1 "If you like this kind of food and you are in Japan, you wanna remember that every area has a local dish, and if you eat it in that area it tastes significantly better. There are places in London that do the same thing, but to me the idea of eating, say, a cow's tongue, is disgusting wherever you are."

He looked around the room as if to continue the debate but everyone was still fixated on the beer/hand-relief business.

Man 1 (moving towards the kitchen) "Anybody for a drink?"

No one responded.

John Lewis

Eavesdropping, like so many aspects of our existence, has been transformed by the ubiquity of the mobile phone. Strangers now think nothing of conversing loudly in public about matters that would have once been whispered in private, as long as they're on the phone. And while this yields the odd astonishing insight into their otherwise secret lives, more often than not these semi-conversations are an unwanted, over-loud reminder of the underlying banality of our existence.

It was a slice of rare tedium indeed that was served to the upstairs passengers on a No. 8 bus recently, as one of their number attempted to organize his friends over the phone.

Man "He's outside John Lewis, blud. I'll be there in… he should be coming towards you… stay where you are!" He frantically keyed in another number. "He's outside H&M, coming towards you… I'm on the bus." Then his other phone rang. "MY PHONE'S RINGING!" he yelled. "I'll call you back… you on the payphone? Don't move, stay where you are… I'm on a bus." It rang again. "Where are you now? *You're by John Lewis?* Well you must have passed him! Go back – listen, my phone's ringing… Hello, you missed him!"

I searched silently for reasons why any of this should matter. There were none. They all had phones, why didn't they speak to each other? The area in question seemed to be small enough. Why not just arrange to meet at a certain place and time and go there? No, it seemed they had surrendered their independence to top-deck traffic-control man, and must suffer the consequences. "Go *BACK* to John Lewis! I AM TELLING YOU I AM ON THE BUS. HELLO? STAY where you *ARE*!"

Locker

While eye contact can be a serious business in swimming-pool changing rooms, keeping your ears open is a far less perilous affair. It was in one of these locker rooms that, as befits the curious etiquette of such environments, two men who only knew each other slightly bumped into each other and fell into uneasy conversation.

Man 1 (of oriental extraction) "Hello!"

Man 2 (in a Birmingham accent, speaking slowly in the classic "I will enable foreigners to understand me" style) "I – am – fine. How – are – you?"

Man 1 (in perfect English) "Oh, I am great. Enjoying my stay."

Man 2 (realizing his mistake and amending his delivery slightly) "Have you got any plans? For the weekend?"

Man 1 "Yes, I've bought a bicycle. I thought I might cycle to Stonehenge. Is it far?"

Man 2 "Oh, about two hundred miles, I think."

This was either a chronic overestimate of around a hundred and fifty miles or – as it transpired – in an absurd fit of regional pride, Man 2 was about to try and trick Man 1 into visiting Birmingham instead.

Man 1 (undeterred) "That's good. Is there a town nearby where I could stay?"

Man 2 (trying to cover up the existence of Salisbury) "No. It's completely isolated. There aren't any towns."

Man 1 "A hotel?"

Man 2 "No hotels either. The facilities are very basic. It's neolithic. Have you thought about going to Birmingham?"

Man 1 "Birmingham?"

Man 2 "Yeah, it's much closer." (another lie) "And you can cycle all the way there on the canals."

Man 1 "Canals?"

Man 2 "Oh yeah, more canals than Venice!"

Man 1 "I think I want to go to Stonehenge first."

Man 2 (implying that he would face death at the hands of druids if he did so) "Yeah, well that's your lookout. Don't say I didn't warn you."

And with that he moved off, perhaps to cleanse himself of his deception in the showers.

Respect Bus

The bus was already unbearably hot and damp thanks to that peculiar collective courtesy that stops anyone opening windows on wet, cold days. As the passengers sat and steamed, the atmosphere of vague discomfort was ratcheted up into mild panic by that most unwelcome of outbursts – a tirade of loud swearing from a gang of unruly teens on the back seats.

Teen 1 (sounding genuinely angry) "Get the fuck off me, blud. I ain't saying it again. Don't fuckin' push me too far now!"

Like everyone else, I pretended to keep on reading the evening paper, while wondering what direction this would go and how best to stay as uninvolved as possible.

Teen 2 (in a reassuring tone) "Calm yourself down."

Teen 1 (slightly calmer) "Then stop taking photos of me!"

It was then that a third voice emerged and addressed itself to the image-conscious delinquent.

Teen 3 (with great authority) "Why don't you stop swearing on the bus and respect the public?"

Teen 1 (indignant) "What public, what you on about?"

Teen 3 (patiently) "It's public transport innit."

Teen 1 (pausing whilst reading the bus logo then announcing triumphantly) "It says London Transport!"

Teen 3 (loud enough to get everyone's attention, though he had it anyway) "Everybody, I want you to come up the back here and give this boy a slap!"

I took a risk at this point and looked around. Teen 3 was huge, Teen 1 was fuming and Teen 2 was about to take another picture with his phone.

Teen 1 "Leave me alone!"

Teen 3 "You should respect the public like they're respecting you."

We're not respecting him, I thought, we're scared. But it didn't seem like an appropriate moment to get pedantic. So I got back to the paper and waited to see if this uneasy truce would hold.

Mercenary

First warm evening of the year and, before you can put your pint glass on the pavement, out come the freaks. Two men had been forced into polite intimacy while their mutual acquaintance went back inside the pub to buy a round. After an uncomfortable silence, the smaller of the two – who was dressed in a suit – began speaking to the other, whose look hovered somewhere between ex-military issue and sexual ambiguity.

Man 1 (reluctantly) "So, as a mercenary, you make good money."

Man 2 (with pride) "Shitloads. When you negotiate your services, you've got to know what to ask for."

Man 1 "Do you enjoy it?"

Man 2 "Well, I wouldn't say *enjoy*. I have no respect for officers. Basically, it's an officer's job to get you killed. My job is to say 'Right, let's get in, do the job, get out' – and get paid. I have no time for officers. Although I was actually an officer."

Man 1 (interested now) "You can be one, even as a mercenary?"

Man 2 "Yeah. It's exactly the same system. I made it to captain. As a mercenary it works the same, although you are never part of the army."

I had to nip inside the pub for a moment, and when I came out Man 2 had taken the exchange to a different level.

Man 2 "So, basically, you never tell good jokes. A bad joke can really help you in those sorts of situations. I personally have memorized thousands of really bad jokes. When you tell a good joke, people just think, 'Who is this smart-arse?' You tell a bad joke, and they feel sorry for you. They want to be your friend."

Man 1 (transfixed) "When did you last use one of them?"

Man 2 "In Vietnam. Not in the war. But I needed to negotiate with a tribe. I – er – told them a bad joke. They got to like me, and I got away. It was handy, because quite often I can intimidate people without even realizing it."

I finished my drink and had no further excuse to loiter, but as I returned my glass to the bar I noted that events were about to enter a spiritual dimension.

"Oh, no, no," said Man 2 emphatically. "Don't get me started on that. Now, Buddhism. That's a whole different ball game."

Phone Panic

We all have different ideas about what constitutes an emergency. For one young man finishing breakfast with his girlfriend in a café the fact that her mobile had run out of power constituted a crisis of such dimensions that it seemed reasonable to assume that they hadn't known each other all that long.

Man (in the melodramatic style of someone in a day-time soap receiving news of an infidelity) "Your phone's dead?" (then calming himself down) "OK, right. Let me call Charlie. I'm calling Charlie…"

The woman stared at him as he punched the numbers into his phone. Then he nodded at her reassuringly as he put the handset to his ear.

Man "Charlie! How are you mate? Yeah, I know how it is… Listen, got a bit of a problem, you know Wendy… yeah, well we need to come round and charge up her phone… just round the corner. Have you got a Nokia charger?… But you know what one looks like yeah?" (then looking to the woman) "Is it a new one or an old one?"

Woman (puzzled) "I don't know."

Man (to Charlie) "She doesn't know. It looks pretty new. Why don't we just pop round... oh you're at the studio. Cool. How long will you be there for? Oh wicked. Oh well never mind. OK I'll see you later."

Woman "It really doesn't matter, I can wait."

Man (oblivious to her plea and beckoning towards the waitress and doing a sort of mime with his phone) "Hey, excuse me, have you got a Nokia charger? No? They haven't got one."

Woman "It's fine."

Man "I'll think of something."

Rave Toilet

Visiting a bar that appeared to be relatively civilized, I was surprised to discover that it shared a bathroom with what appeared to be a full-scale, old-fashioned rave taking place in the basement. The scenes inside were disturbing to say the least: sweat-drenched men in T-shirts bent over trying to suck moisture from broken taps, others pulling faces in the mirror and asking themselves if they were all right, and so on. Taking my place at the urinal and staring firmly at the wall, I initially assumed the man to my left was talking to someone else.

Man (in a loud, well-spoken voice) "I am absolutely rogered."

An unfortunate choice of euphemism, considering the circumstances, but I thought no more of it and focused on the tiling.

Man (even louder) "Absolutely rogered in this area tonight!"

I could sense in my peripheral vision that he was looking at me now, and lost the will to piss completely.

Man (growling like a bad Barry White impersonator) "Oooooh yeah."

I decided to cut my losses and began doing up my fly.

Man "Back to the battlefield, eh?"

I looked at him and he nodded towards my under-wear, as luck would have it a pair of battered Union Jack boxer shorts.

Man "Patriot, are you?"

Me "Someone gave them to me."

Man "Got any pills?"

Me "Why, what's wrong with you?"

Man (gripping the urinal as though it were a pinball machine and grimacing) "You know the score!"

I made to leave and he spun round towards me.

Man "You wanna chill out a bit!"

Indeed, and you wanna put your genitals away and get yourself home, I thought as I walked away.

"Go on!" he yelled. It was the first sensible thing he'd said all evening.

Cricket

Three days before the now infamous England-Pakistan test match was abandoned, I was in the stands next to three guys in their sixties sporting carcinogenic suntans and thick gold jewellery. During a lull in play the crowd's attention was diverted by the sight and sound of an enormous Chinook helicopter flying over the ground.

Man 1 "Look at that. Marvellous innit."

Man 2 (as though he had been disappointed by smaller aircraft all day) "Now *that* is a fucking helicopter."

Man 3 "Tell you what, you wouldn't want them rotors to get out of sync."

Man 1 "Too right."

Man 3 "You know the Spitfire, right? No Spitfire *ever* crashed due to mechanical failure."

Man 2 (preparing to disagree) "Say that again?"

Man 3 "In the war, no Spitfires went down cos of engine failure."

Man 1 "You're saying they were all shot down."

Man 3 "That's what I'm saying. Those that we lost were all shot down."

Man 2 "How do you know?"

Man 3 "It's documented."

Man 2 "Bollocks. What, you mean to say, every time one got shot down, the pilot, as he hurtles towards the earth, radios in and says, 'Control, this is red leader, been shot down over the Rhine – death imminent. Just wanted to confirm it was the Germans that got me, and not engine failure.'"

Man 3 (realizing that the credibility of his argument was also losing altitude) "No, well I'm not saying that…"

Man 2 "No, no you're not saying anything, are you, you're making it up."

Man 3 (laughing) "Well it sounded good, didn't it."

Man 2 "Oh yeah, you went right up in my estimation."

Man 1 "There you go then."

Man 3 "I never liked you anyway."

Shoe Conkers

Waiting for a train to leave the station, I noticed a well-dressed couple across the aisle, the precise nature of whose relationship remained obscure, save for the fact that the man was clearly in thrall to the woman.

Woman (sitting at a table and neatly arranging a laptop and a series of newspapers and magazines) "He was wearing gingham, so I was... well you can imagine..."

Man (standing over her) "Well that's the thing about him isn't it? He's a very good egg. There's an air of pomposity about him, but it's a mask."

Woman "A mask of pomposity!"

Man "Indeed, a mask, and behind it he really is an excellent chap."

Woman (wistfully) "His shoes were the colour of conkers. Thanks for everything."

Man "Thank you. Safe journey."

He leant over and kissed her on the cheek in a way that was neither intimate nor entirely unfamiliar. He left the carriage and looked through the window. They placed their hands against each other's through the glass in the manner of prison visitors. She held up her computer, which had a picture of a young baby as its screen saver.

Woman (loudly, slowly and with extra vivid movements of her lips) "I've just bought him his first pair of wellingtons!"

If he was the father, he would know that, I thought to myself. He stood on the platform, wiping his nose, looking as confused about his role in the scheme of things as I was.

Woman (with the kind of "wrap up warm" gesture one might use with children or the elderly) "Keep your scarf on!"

He waved the end of it back at her as the train moved out, and looked like he would never take it off.

Snake Builder

Early morning in a café, and three builders, so dusty that they'd either already put a good day's work in or woken up in yesterday's clothes, ordered breakfasts of unfeasible magnitude before discussing their plans for the weekend.

Builder 1 (in an abrupt cockney accent) "Whatchyou-doin' for Easter?"

Builder 2 (with a pronounced Midlands twang) "I've got to look for a snake."

Builder 1 (alarmed and incredulous) "A snake?"

Builder 2 (deadpan) "It's loose in my house."

Builder 1 "Is it poisonous?"

Builder 2 "It is if it bites you."

Builder 1 (with genuine horror, as though his colleague were admitting to something contemptible) "What *sort* of snake?"

Builder 2 (folding up his newspaper to emphasize the increased seriousness of their exchange) "It's an African grass snake. It got out before, but we found it behind the radiator. It likes the heat."

There was a long pause while Builder 1 looked at Builder 2 as if he were seeing him for the first time.

Builder 2 (unfazed) "The weird thing is it rolls itself up into an S-shape before it strikes. When a snake bites, you don't feel it as much as you might expect. If a hamster bites you, it hurts more. The snake is very fast, almost gentle. The hamster's bite is more blunt."

There was another silence.

Builder 2 "The missus ain't too chuffed, but the kids actually look forward to it. It beats an egg anyway, I reckon."

Builder 1 was having none of it, and stared off towards the kitchen, hoping perhaps that the arrival of his breakfast would make the whole unlikely business go away.

Social Work

At seven o'clock on a summer's evening, a group of friends had gathered outside a pub and were discussing their working day. While it transpired that most of them languished in nondescript media jobs, one man's tale of life on the front lines of the social services soon emerged as the dominant anecdote.

Man (with perverse pride) "I tell you, our office is a shambles, and the people that work there are just as bad. If I went on a visit and found someone's house in the state that office is in, I'd have 'em taken into care for their own good!"

Much laughter from friends at this.

Man (warming to his theme) "I gave up using the fridge long ago. It is absolutely fucking foul, proper health scare. No one else is bothered. That's not all, they *steal* the spoons! I swear to you. People keep them locked in their desks or in their pockets, and if you put one down – bang! – that's that. You try and make a cup of tea, ask for a spoon and everybody looks away. And these are care workers!"

Friend (wiping tears of laughter from his eyes) "Man, that is so not right."

Man (shaking his head) "That ain't the half of it. Some of them don't even answer the phone. The other day I see one girl I work with is wearing headphones and staring at her laptop while the phone's ringing. I figure maybe she's working on something, and then I walk behind her and she's watching a fucking DVD!"

Friend (reasonably certain that he'll never need to contact social services in his life) "Man, that is just too much."

Celery Boy

Grabbing some lunch, I noticed that the man on the next table was making specific nutritional demands of the waitress about salad.

Man (dressed casually, but with a look on his face that said that when it came to salad he was deadly serious) "No celery in that salad."

Waitress (dutifully noting it down) "No celery."

Man 2 (puzzled at his friend's request) "What's up with that?"

Man 1 "I can't stand it."

Man 2 "But it's mostly water."

Man 1 (visibly troubled) "It's not the taste…"

Man 2 "What then?"

Man 1 "God, it's a long story. Years ago my boss sent me out to buy some. I'd never bought celery before. I found a bunch in the shop, broke a stick off and went to pay for it. The woman at the till told me that I had to buy the whole bunch."

Man 1 "And that's it?"

Man 2 "Hell no. This was a small town. The next day I found out that she'd phoned my boss, *from her fucking house*, to tell him what I'd done. There wasn't much to talk about at my work, so they started calling me 'Celery Boy'. It was a butcher's, and they told every customer that came in. It got way out of hand. I was only fourteen. I pulled the kidneys out of dead pigs."

Man 2 "Wow."

Man 1 "It didn't end there. Years later I was in a pub in town, and a much older woman, a big lass, came up to me and said, 'Didn't you use to be Celery Boy?'

"I said. 'Yeah. And you want to try eating it a bit more often.' She went nuts, told her husband and it all got out of hand. It was one of the reasons I left home in the end."

Man 2 (trying to be sympathetic) "Maybe it was all for the best then?"

Man 1 (looking at his salad, unconvinced) "Maybe."

Tall Colleague

In a busy café, two women, who had spent the better part of their lunch break having an unremarkable conversation about children, were distracted by a waitress bringing them some food they had ordered to take away. They looked at the wrapped sandwich and then at each other.

Woman 1 (staring at the package) "We should go, he'll be hungry."

Woman 2 (nodding in agreement) "For someone so tall, though, he is very considerate."

Woman 1 "He does go out of his way not to stand right next to you if you're very small, but then you think *she's* only five foot two."

They paused for a moment to consider the practical and presumably carnal implications of their colleague's great height.

Woman 1 "I think it must be lonely."

Woman 2 "Being that tall?"

Woman 1 "Not just that, but then keeping away from people so that they don't feel small."

Woman 2 (drifting off a little) "You wouldn't want him to get angry."

And then it was as though their vast associate's shadow had fallen across the room as they busied themselves and began to leave with a sense of great purpose. Whether unable to buy his own lunch out of height shame or mere practicality, it was clear now that, like a nursery-rhyme giant, it was important to keep him fed and happy. It was a small café, and it felt as though everyone in it was now aware that in some nearby office a very tall man was growing hungry and looking at his watch.

Woman 1 "Better get a move on."

Woman 2 "Have you ever seen him dance?"

Kill and Eat

Certain conversations seem to belong to another place entirely from where you actually hear them. The following exchange between a young American student type and a kind of survivalist Bill Oddie seemed particularly inappropriate for pre-lunch drinks in a pub in London.

American "What did you kill?"

Wild Bill "Deer, antelope. You've got to know what you're doing."

American "I heard that if you shoot a deer in the wrong place, in the heart or something, it bleeds internally and spoils the meat so you can't eat it. Is that true?"

Wild Bill (dismissively) "Bullshit. You've got to hack off all the limbs, then the meat's OK. Depends what part you want to eat. The key to killing a deer – shoot it in the neck. It starts running around like crazy. But, very important, you've got to stand perfectly still for half an hour. Wait for it to run itself out. When it collapses, you've got to move in and start preparing the meat immediately."

American (wide-eyed and credulous) "What do you do?"

Wild Bill "It's all in the cutting. There's two styles. The first one" (starts making a slicing motion in the air) "is *vertical*, in line with the meat. That's your jerky style. That's the way you may have had it."

American (sadly) "I've never had deer."

Wild Bill "Well the other way, that's the way if you're in the bush, to make the meat last. It's to cut *across* the meat." (more cutting motions) "It stems the blood. That way, the meat lasts for incredible amounts of time. Very important when you're on your own in the bush. Could be months before your next kill."

American "So what was the longest you ever kept a piece of meat?"

Wild Bill (after a thoughtful pause) "Eight years."

I threw back my pint and left, thinking that TV survivalists have a lot to answer for.

Museum Judgement

In the cafeteria of a famous museum I heard voices coming from the table behind me that sounded so antiquated and refined that at first I thought they might be part of an audio-visual exhibit on vanished dialects.

Woman "Well, you're aware that he appeared at my house at ten in the morning, clutching a bottle of wine?"

Man (sounding affirmative via a mouthful of food) "Mmmmmmmgggn."

Woman "He says he's depressed and that he's tired of being on his own! I said, 'Well I'm on my own and I couldn't be happier.' But he honestly said to me that he doesn't care if he lives or dies."

Man "Knew a fellow like that in the army."

At this point I was compelled to turn and look at them. Expecting the man to resemble the Major from *Fawlty Towers*, I was shocked to see that he was probably no older than thirty-five, though dressed in tweed and with wild orange hair, like a well-bred clown. I figured the woman must be his mother, seeing as she was dabbing crumbs from his mouth with a napkin.

Woman "I went over to his place – you remember that apartment – and the dust was inches thick! I tried to clean up, but of course it's futile. He won't do anything for himself, and eventually I got quite cross. He was just sitting there, growing a beard in his bloody underwear all day, and I said, "Why don't you read a book, or go outside, go to a museum and take an interest in something? Get a hobby!"

As motivational speeches went, it was pretty poor stuff. I got out of the museum as quickly as I could, and began work on a beard of my own.

Boxes

In the loading bay of a business with no discernible purpose, two men were shifting small mountains of packages about, when they fell into a dispute.

Man 1 (sporting dreadlocks and a South African accent) "Hey! Hey, man! I don't get paid any more for picking up your boxes you know!"

The other man walked away nonchalantly from his colleague and the box he had just dumped at his feet.

Man 1 (standing up fully to reveal a T-shirt that had "SHUT UP!" written on it in big letters) "What, you think I'm fucking joking here? I'm not touching it. Get it out of my way!"

Man 2 (returning with another box and leaving it) "They ain't my boxes."

Man 1 (pointing in an accusatory way at the packages) "This is bloody out of order! Do you want me to tell Graham?"

Man 2 (lighting a cigarette and sitting on a crate) "Tell who you like."

Man 1 (running out of options and beginning to move the boxes) "This is no way to treat people, man. You're bloody sick."

Man 2 (pointing at him with his fag) "You got a fucked-up attitude, you know that?"

Man 1 "Yeah, and who made me that way? People like you who don't know how to behave, how to treat another human being."

Man 2 (now bursting an enormous sheet of bubble wrap between his fingers) "Shut up about it."

With that he gave what was left of his cigarette to his colleague and began to shift boxes himself.

Man 1 (smoking and shaking his head) "I'll put you in a bloody box one of these days, man."

Man 2 "Yeah, yeah."

Burger Hags

In fast-food restaurants you become accustomed to the sight and sound of groups of youngsters loudly expressing themselves around tables and generally making the experience even more hellish than it is anyway. It was especially shocking then to enter one on a Saturday afternoon to find it dominated in an equally aggressive and foul-mouthed manner by a group of women, none of whom appeared to be a day under seventy.

Woman 1 (clearly their leader) "I sees 'em coming. They come up to me and I tell 'em to fuck right off."

Women 2, 3 and 4 (staring into styrofoam cups and stirring their contents like witches in the McDonald's production of *Macbeth*) "Yeah, you tell 'em."

Woman 1 "Speaking of seeing things, when he died, I swear I could see his eyes moving when he was lying there in the front room. I looked at him and he looked back at me!"

Woman 2 "In his coffin?"

Woman 1 "In his bleedin' coffin!"

Woman 3 "I ain't havin' that."

Woman 1 "Well it never happened did it, but you never know."

They sat in contemplation of the supernatural for a moment until Woman 3 picked up a newspaper.

Woman 1 "What's on tonight then?"

Woman 3 (with seasoned resignation) "Saturday innit, fuck all."

It was then that an employee, having failed to take stock of the raw matriarchal power of the table, moved in to tidy up the remnants of their meal.

Woman 1 "You leave that be, girl!"

Sensing that there was almost three hundred years of combined and malign wisdom focused against her, she wisely backed off towards the sulking and emasculated teens across the room.

Clock on a Stick

By a pelican crossing in Camden Town two young artisans covered in white paint and plaster dust were berating a passing flock of German goths who looked almost as pale as they were.

Man 1 (more of a joke than a threat) "Oi, gutentag, gutentag, how are yer?"

The tourists shuffled past in an orderly monochrome crocodile, saying nothing.

Man 2 (half-heartedly) "Gutentag."

Man 1 (suddenly losing interest in the Germans and becoming incredulous of the entire city) "Why do they come 'ere, what the fuck for? Look at it, there's nothing here, the place is a shithole. Why would you bother? I mean Houses of Parliament? Big Ben? Just a building! If you were gonna go somewhere you'd go to Egypt wouldn't yer? See them things, what they called?"(making angry triangular shapes in the air with his hands) "Pyramids! What are they *for*, bruv? What are they *about*?"

Man 2 (considerably less agitated) "Tombs innit."

Man 1 (exasperated now and beginning to cause unease amongst fellow pedestrians) "Big Ben! What is it? It's just a clock on a stick innit? A fuckin' tower!"

Man 2 (deadpan) "It's the bell."

Man 1 "Eh?"

Man 2 "Big Ben is the name of the bell."

Man 1 (having none of it) "You what?"

Man 2 "Don't worry about it."

Man 1 "Call it what you want, it's bollocks, it's a clock."

I was on the point of asking him what he thought of the Olympic bid, but the lights changed and the city in which he saw so little merit swallowed him up again.

Bookmark

The hubbub of another night's outdoor drinking was interrupted by the cries of a young street entrepreneur/ vagrant in dated New Age traveller attire who approached the pub with a unique offer.

Man "Sorry to bother you, but would anybody like a bookmark or some sculpture?"

He was holding a coil of bent brass wire, from which it seemed either of these items could be made. There was a moment of quiet while people assessed the situation.

Man "Look, I won't mess you about, I'm homeless, yeah? And rather than walking around begging or whatever, I thought I'd try offering something in return. This is what I do. I make sculptures and bookmarks. Does anybody want one in return for a donation?"

I wondered if perhaps I actually did need a bookmark, whilst worrying that someone might try and say something clever that would make the whole situation worse. Luckily no one did, and he moved on to the people behind.

Man "Anybody want a bookmark or some sculpture?"

Assembled drinkers "No thanks, you're all right."

It was then that one of the group, rather than taking refuge in their collective response, felt compelled to justify his refusal.

Drinking man "Actually, you wouldn't believe this, but I'm actually begging myself! I've left my wallet... all my cards in the office... so I actually don't have any money."

Bookmark man "If you want something, maybe someone could lend you some money?"

Drinking man's friend (sensing an opportunity to humiliate him) "Yeah, I'll lend you some money, how many bookmarks did you have in mind?"

Bookmark man "Yeah, how many?"

Drinking man "Well I'm not actually... actually reading... anything at the moment... oh that's my phone."

He made a bad job of pretending to take a phone call and started walking away. There was widespread laughter, especially from bookmark man, as he marched out of sight.

Cat Eater

I was having a cup of tea in a café that was closing up for the afternoon when an almost spherical woman of indeterminate age in big, thick glasses stuck her head round the door and began asking strange things of the proprietor.

Woman (gesturing with her head at the owner's mop) "'Ere, do you want any help, for free, unpaid?"

Owner (evidently familiar with this sort of thing) "No love, you're all right."

Woman "You know me, I used to have all kinds of money, now I'm going bankrupt. A cheque's gone missing. The postman won't do nothing about it. I dunno where to turn."

Owner (trying to tune it all out) "Hmmmn."

Woman (clearly singing from her own hymn sheet) "Do you think I'll get that bird flu from the dog?"

Owner "Eh?"

At this point the chef appeared and began to pay attention.

Woman "Do you think it's gonna rain? I haven't seen the cat in ages…"

Chef (moving to diffuse the situation) "No, well you wouldn't. We've had that. It come in 'ere and we cooked it. He" – pointing at me – "had the last of it. What did you think?"

They all turned and stared. There are times when you can slot right into this type of discourse. But this wasn't one of them. So I sort of smiled, which seemed to satisfy everyone except the woman. I emptied my mug and stood up.

Me "Thanks for the tea."

The woman stared at me as though I might feasibly have eaten her pet. Then she disappeared. I looked to the staff for reassurance, and the chef said, to no one in particular, "Another day in paradise." Which was all the explanation I needed.

Deal or No Deal

Entering a pub I had not visited for years, I was stunned to find the entire clientele glued to Noel Edmonds's *Deal or No Deal* on the widescreen TV. From the rapt attention of the gaggle of retirement-age/unemployable drinkers, it was clear this was no accident, and the show was an integral part of their routine.

Man 1 (wearing a blazer and shouting at the screen) "Take the money!"

Barman (having downed tools for the occasion) "No deal!"

Edmonds (disconcertingly life-size on the giant screen) "The banker wants you to go, he wants to be the victor."

Man 2 (lapsing in and out of consciousness while standing, and looking like he could fight you in his sleep) "Fucking deal, man!"

Edmonds "It's a £20,000 cash offer."

Man 1 "Take it!"

Edmonds "Reg would have liked £20,000 yester-day…"

Man 2 "Fuck Reg!"

Edmonds "I'm not sure we've been in this position before."

Man 3 (pausing on his way to the urinal in case he missed anything) "He says that every day!"

Edmonds "Park your ego. Is it deal or no deal?"

Man 2 "Deal fuck!"

Contestant "Deal."

Edmonds "This is the point where everything changes…"

Man 1 (with great authority) "There's nothing in there!" It transpired that the contestant had made a smart move and won some money. "I knew it, I told you."

The brief social coherence the show provided ended with the arrival of the adverts, yet the TV stayed on, doubtless in anticipation of *Richard and Judy's Wine Club*.

Black Country Express

On an intercity train already rendered unbearable by overcrowding and an air-conditioning failure, a young woman added to the climate of justifiable homicide by yelling the details of her recent life into her phone.

Woman "How random is that? I'm going down to London to see Mark! Don't worry, if he doesn't meet with your approval he's going anyway!"

I looked to see if this was a deliberate broadcast, but she seemed quite unaware of the existence of her audience and its growing hostility.

Woman "We should all go out in Solihull! I'll scout out the boys in London to save us both coming down. That way you should find someone easy, if I don't pull them first. Get this though, I've got a massive cold sore and I've come out in spots!"

She was right about the spots. The cold sore, though, as is often the way with such anxieties, was barely noticeable.

Woman "And I bought the new Harry Potter and I've not brought it with me! Two hours I'm on this train, two hours with nothing to read!"

This wasn't strictly true, poking from the top of her Marilyn Monroe handbag was a magazine with the headline 'Sad Kerry Finds Love'.

Woman "Still I've got my make-up to do, that'll take a while."

The reception was dwindling so she repeated herself with added volume.

Woman "I SAID I'LL DO MY MAKE-UP, THAT'LL TAKE A WHILE!"

With that the signal died and she did indeed proceed to put on her make-up. So much so that she eventually attained a kind of corn-fed appearance, a look that Mark in London was no doubt powerless to resist.

Bus Labours Lost

On a bus an unlikely pair of young men, one a solid cockney type, the other with dyed blond hair and an American accent, discussed their plans for future employment with an air of fatalism and a complete absence of career-mindedness that was heartening to behold.

Man 1 (the Londoner) "Why don't you get a live-in pub job?"

Man 2 (unimpressed) "I'd rather kill myself. There's no way I could deal with that. I get sacked all the time anyway."

Man 1 (evidently the voice of experience) "You should walk out before you get sacked. Don't give 'em the satisfaction. You should get a job in a music shop."

Man 2 (sounding less than keen) "How?"

Man 1 "Just ask in the shops."

Man 2 (shaking his head) "I can't do it. I'm out five nights a week anyway. There's no point even trying."

Man (as though recalling a golden age) "I had a job

in Clinton Cards – *that* was a great job. Nice hours, not stressful. I tell you. It – is – not – stressful."

Man 2 (as though recalling a nightmare) "I worked in Safeways for two hours once. You had to memorize stuff. Till codes and shit. I couldn't handle it. I freaked and they had to let me go."

Man 1 "Not any more. They scan stuff."

Man 2 (suddenly excited) "I could do that."

Man 1 (with laidback optimism) "They train you up."

Man 2 (coming to his senses) "No, no. I'd get sacked."

I sneaked a look back at him and figured he was probably right.

Unlucky Man

It was midweek rush hour, and an incident on the tube had forced people out of the underground and onto the already crowded buses. As around a dozen people within earshot of where I was sitting phoned their offices to explain their lateness, it became clear that the man next to me was having a far worse day than anyone else. First he phoned his office.

Man "Someone's gone under a train at Liverpool Street and the whole line's down. I'm gonna be another half an hour."

Then he phoned an insurance company, gave out policy numbers and a car registration and explained that, "I ain't got no crime number yet. I know the name of the officer that's dealing with it... around eleven o'clock last night."

But it was his third call that tied everything together.

Man "Oh, they jacked it out of nowhere man, they came from nowhere! I dropped her off, I'm on her mother's driveway. She'd just gone inside. There was a

hand on my mouth, a hand round my neck and bang!
– it was over. They'll probably just dump it, you know.
I had a full tank as well!"

To his credit, he was actually laughing by this point.

"I don't need it, I do not need it! No man needs that.
Now I'm on a bus, and when I get in I gotta do a policy
audit… and my boiler's gone as well!"

So, to sum up, a suicide made him late for work, he'd
had his car stolen violently, his boiler had packed up
and he worked in insurance. In a more polite society I
might have turned and commiserated with him. Instead
I just sat there, and wondered if he'd made the whole
thing up.

Carpet Scream

Most days when the weather's warm I walk past a window from which obscenities are hurled – often at me, but lately I was stopped in my tracks by an outburst of such volume and ferocity that it seemed almost superhuman.

Woman's voice 1 (rising in volume from a mild yell) "Don't blame me! I said don't you blame me, Ma!" (then peaking with operatic force) "I AIN'T THE ONE WHO JUST COME BACK FROM DUBAI WITH A FARSAND PAHND CARPET!!!"

There was the kind of silence that follows sounds of great magnitude, before it began again.

Woman's voice 1 "She's always been jealous of me."

Woman's voice 2 "Somehow she thinks she's better than anyone else."

Woman's voice 1 "You don't know, Mum, I know who I am!"

Woman's voice 2 "I know you do."

Woman's voice 1 "I might be an arsehole, but I've always been there for her. Ever since she was a baby she's had whatever she wanted – and it ain't no cheap shit neither. That proper hurt me, what she said. She's got no mates, sitting around, eating pizza in front of people. I've told her she ain't going out in no vest top, but off she goes."

Woman's voice 2 "How is she at school?"

Woman's voice 1 "Fine. I ain't worried about her SATs scores, cos I know she's clever."

Woman's voice 2 "What about that thing?"

Woman's voice 1 "I told her to go in and tell the teacher your mum says 'bollocks'."

Woman's voice 2 "And he hasn't shown his face?"

Woman's voice 1 "No. And I'd stuff his carpet up his arse if he did!"

If he was lucky, I thought, he might even have some carpet left over to stick in his ears.

Launderette

The only good thing about a broken washing machine is that it propels you back into one of the best eavesdropping venues of all: the launderette. On the day I went in, such was the height of the air temperature combined with the heat of the dryers that the management had thoughtfully placed some chairs outside, enabling a Sesame-Street-style pavement culture to spring up around the place, and it was there that I heard the following exchange.

Woman 1 (with such passion that at first I assumed she had survived some form of chemical attack) "Oh, the air in there was so sweet! I tell you I could not breathe. It was so thick you could taste it. I swear to you I thought I was gonna fall down on the floor it was so bad!"

Woman 2 "What is her problem?"

Woman 1 "I dunno, but I tell you what is a problem. If she puts any more air fresheners in that house, the council is gonna be on to her, the neighbour's gonna be sick, someone's pet is gonna die."

Woman 2 "Man that's wrong!"

Woman 1 "You're telling me it's wrong. But she doesn't even want to open a window. I go all through there – with my eyes watering, I swear – opening 'em up, and then she's coming round behind me closing them. It ain't just them little air fresheners that sit around neither: after you been in she's running round with one of them cans. I tell you I don't know how she survives."

Woman 2 "She must have got used to it."

Woman 1 "She's immune. The only good thing is I don't worry about burglars or nothing no more. Anyone breaks into that house without a gas mask they gonna be dead before they hit the floor."

Woman 2 (laughing) "Do you think that's why she does it?"

Woman 1 (deadpan) "No. She says it's to fight germs."

Caviar

In the departure lounge at Heathrow airport, a scene of professional ineptitude was unfolding like a twenty-first-century Norman Wisdom film. On what was presumably his first day as dogsbody at luxury seafood concession Caviar House, a young man was ordered by his boss to assist a woman who had spilt her child's drink on the nearby concourse.

Boss (as though overseeing a crisis of great magnitude) "Help her! Help her! Take napkins and help her!"

With an eagerness to please that would prove his undoing, the man then seized as many napkins as it is possible to fit in one hand.

Boss (sensing that napkin use on such a scale might dent profits) "No! No! Too many napkins!"

Terrified, the man then dropped some on the floor.

Boss "Argh!"

Both men then scrabbled to collect them, each hindering the efforts of the other. Having assessed the ideal number of napkins for the job, the boss then handed them to the man and directed him back towards the woman, who had since cleared up the accident on her own. Undaunted, the man offered her the napkins.

Boss "No! No! Come back."

Without a crisis, the boss's primary concern was now how best to occupy his hapless underling.

Man "What should I do?"

Boss (suppressing the urge to say "Resign!" and handing him a cloth instead) "Clean up."

Man "What should I clean?"

Boss "Anything!"

The man looked around him and eventually began wiping a pillar in a forlorn way.

Boss "Faster, come on, look busy."

He had a point. It was almost enough to put you off your oysters.

Chanel

There is a shop in London that takes its transactions so seriously that on the moment of purchase you are invited into a private room to be parted from your money. I was waiting outside in a state of benign delusion over my finances when an assistant ran into the room and emerged with one of her colleagues.

Assistant 1 (in the kind of pan-European accent popular in shops where a pair of shoes can cost more than a second-hand car) "That handbag is £900 – the deposit is £250, not £100!"

Assistant 2 "Oh no! You tell him."

They went into the room together.

Assistant 1 "I'm sorry sir, the bag is £900, so the deposit is £250."

Man 1 (sounding elderly, pompous and a bit pickled) "Well I only have £100 on me. Surely that will do? I'll be in on Monday with the rest, and failing that the money's yours. What difference does it make?"

Assistant 1 "I'm sorry but there is a system…"

Man 1 (up on his hind legs, verbally speaking) "I don't care about the system, surely it's up to you. Have you no power? No authority?"

Assistant 1 (unintimidated) "It's not a question of power sir, or a question of my authority. It is the way we do things here."

Man 1 "Well that's absurd. I don't suppose you could help me out?"

Man 2 (evidently a shopping accomplice) "I don't see why not."

Man 1 (becoming cooperative) "When I return, can you refund my friend's deposit and allow me to make up the full amount myself? Would you be happy with that?"

Assistant 1 (with awesome monotonic authority) "It's not a question of *my* happiness sir, *you* are the customer, it is about *your* happiness."

The men completed their transactions and emerged looking like scolded children, far from happy.

Courier

It would be nice to think that your own home might offer some respite from the demented chatter of twenty-first-century life, but it turns out nowhere is safe. The other day I answered a knock at the door only to be subjected to what amounted to an oral happy slap from a cycle courier who appeared clinically compelled to deliver unsolicited anecdotes along with registered packages.

Him "Just sign here."

Me "Thanks."

Him "I love this job."

Me (handing back pen and clipboard) "Good."

Him "I'm glad I came down here. You meet all sorts of people. I just saw a bloke round the corner, hadn't seen him for years. Brilliant!"

Me (sealing my fate with a futile attempt to be convivial while gradually shutting the door) "You didn't owe him any money I hope!"

Him "Nah. I see famous people too. All of 'em. I was in Kensington, right? And I heard this engine…" He makes engine noises. "It was a fucking Porsche, and it's gone past me so I caught up with it, caught it at the lights. Looked in and it's fuckin' Jenson Button. So I knocked on the window and says, 'Oi, Jenson!' And he gives me his autograph and then I thought – you know what, I should have got two, mate. Cos I can sell one then!"

Me (struggling to form a lie) "I've left the gas on…"

Him (undeterred) "Then – then I'm at that parade thing, right in the crowd, and the other driver, Montoya's come past, and there's a Ferrari there too, so I've shouted out, loud as I can, 'Oi, Montoya. Enjoy that Ferrari, cos it's the closest you'll ever get to one!' Oh, dear me. And then the bloke next to me said, 'That's harsh.' And I said, 'No, mate, I am telling it like it is!'"

I nodded, though I knew nothing at all about motor racing. His radio crackled and he sped off, giggling. I looked at the package. It was for the people next door.

Chicken Women

I was drinking with a friend outside a pub by a round-about when a souped-up hatchback skidded to halt and double-parked in front of us. I was surprised when the driver, a young woman, wound down her window and screamed, "You slags!" in our general direction. Mercifully, this turned out to be aimed at the table of women behind us, hitherto unremarkable save for the amount of cigarettes they were smoking, given the apparent flammability of their clothes.

Driver (leaving the car) "Watcha doin'?"

Women (as one) "Getting pissed up!"

Driver (moving to the back of the vehicle, oblivious of incoming vehicles swerving round her, with an insane confidence that recalled Robert Duvall's character in *Apocalypse Now*) "I've got a boot full of fried chicken here!"

She didn't have to tell them twice, and the women moved to the car and began indulging in an urban picnic as a queue of irate traffic built behind them.

Woman (waving a chicken leg) "This is better than carnival."

A woman then emerged from the pub and walked unsteadily towards the picnic.

"Who's gonna drive me to the cashpoint?" By way of a compromise one of the others threw her a set of keys, and she got into a car and drove off at high speed.

I was just wondering what kind of urban Amazon kingdom I had stumbled across when a young man walked over to get some chicken, and one of the women punched him in the stomach. I tried to look invisible. Cashpoint woman then returned and parked on the pavement.

Cashpoint woman (tossing back the keys) "The fucking queue's three miles long, I can't be bothered."

The driver then turned up the car stereo to drown out the horns from the growing tailback. After that, you couldn't hear anything except the fearful beating of your own heart.

Oz Dogs

No matter how much money you're prepared to spend in a restaurant, you can never be entirely confident that you won't be forced to digest the conversations of fellow diners as part of the package. The larger the bill, the more noise people feel entitled to make while racking it up. So it was that a gang of well-heeled Antipodeans in a fancy metropolitan eatery – who had already declared their status with cries of "Five mill and I'm out" and " I love De Beers" – moved on to the subject of pet care.

Woman (with gleeful shock) "Some of these kennels are over £100 a *week*! I mean, it's like getting your kids into the best school."

Man 1 (concurring) "You can pay £99 a day for dogs!"

Woman "But you should see the cat place. All the cats are in cages facing a central atrium, and there's birds in the middle!"

Man 1 "They reckon the cats love it."

Man 2 (at immense volume) "That's like locking us up in front of a central atrium full of beer!"

Man 1 (amidst subsiding laughter) "We're the people who paid bloody £4,000 to quarantine the animal for six months."

Woman (warming to her theme) "It's £350 at the dog *dentist*. Can you believe that the vet referred them to a bloody dentist? When *I* go to the dentist it doesn't cost that much! They gave them a general anaesthetic."

Woman 2 "Well you say that, but they do have the best possible anaesthetist."

Which was kind of funny, because if there had been an anaesthetist in the restaurant, right then I would have paid all the money I had to be guided into oblivion like a wealthy pet.

Genius

Taking advantage of one of the last sunny evenings of the summer, a group of friends had gathered at a pub by the banks of the Thames. One had perched himself above the others on the river wall itself, which marked him out as some form of leader. Edging nearer, I became aware that they were debating one of the burning issues of the day – the relative merits of Mr Peter Doherty.

Leader (deadly serious) "I'm not sure he's a genius at the moment, but I do think he will become one. At some point. Definitely. It's all in there."

Man (passionate, and about to construct a metaphor so mixed that no meaning could ever be distilled from it) "I think we've put him on a pedestal – and now that's become a knife edge, which is like a downward spiral and it's we, us, that have sent him there."

Leader (imperiously, like he really knew his onions) "All genius is on that knife edge."

Woman (concurring) "It's like Ian Curtis, or Nirvana."

Woman's Boyfriend (condescending, as only people in relationships can be) "Ian Curtis wasn't in Nirvana!"

Woman "I know that."

Man "It's like, we've said he's a genius and he's gone, 'Right, I'm a genius.'"

Leader "And that's a fucking dangerous thing to do."

Man "You can't say you're a genius."

Leader "Absolutely not."

Boyfriend (in the manner of one announcing a significant truth) "Once you say you are, then that's when you're probably not."

Leader (judgementally) "That's when you've lost it."

Man "I'd be really pissed off if he died."

They nodded in agreement as I slunk away, unable to absorb any more wisdom.

EEC

Ordinarily getting your ears bent by someone else's conversation on public transport is a direct consequence of your fellow travellers' youthful exuberance. So for once it was a relief – comparatively speaking – to get on a train next to a group of shouting pensioners. Three men dressed like an upper-middle-class tribute to *Last of the Summer Wine* were dissecting the finer points of European economic policy while their wives whispered amongst themselves, presumably about another matter entirely.

Man 1 (as though reading an obituary for the whole of mankind) "You got German apples, Spanish water and Russian electricity!"

Man 2 (shaking his head) "Russian electricity!"

Man 3 (implying that he had seen all this coming decades ago) "Well you can trace the whole thing back to the origins of the EEC."

Man 1 "Bloody Ted Heath!"

Man 3 "We left it too late to get involved of course. There was a time, you know, when France and Germany were on their uppers and everything was there for the taking, but of course nothing happened. We missed our opportunity and it's been too late ever since."

Man 2 "I tell you where they've got it good. Ireland. There's a hundred thousand millionaires in Ireland!"

Man 1 "Most of what I have is tied up in PEPs. I prefer to move small amounts of money around. I can't check the markets every day. Of course if you're very wealthy it's a different story."

Man 3 "That's what I'm saying, as a country we missed our chance."

Man 1 "Well, by and large we are a very negative race."

Man 2 (enthusiastically) "And proud of it!"

Man 3 (looking sadly out the window at the passing countryside) "Indeed."

But is it Art?

In an exhibition at one of the country's leading art galleries, the usual silence was broken by a female curator crying, "There's a stain on the floor!" in a worried way. The source of her discomfort proved to be a trail of brownish-red matter of no discernible origin. Given that this was an exhibition of quite violent images, my immediate reaction was to assume it was blood. The arrival of a second curator sparked a debate that focused on more mundane options.

Curator 1 (optimistically) "It could be chocolate."

Curator 2 (realistically) "It could be shit."

Curator 1 (leaning in towards it and then backing away in fear) "How can we find out?"

Curator 2 (looking around for a culprit, preferably a child) "I dunno. Whatever it is, someone's brat will have dragged it through here."

Curator 1 (starting to giggle) "What shall we do?"

Curator 2 (as though taking control of a great emergency) "Get on the radio. Get a cleaner up here."

Curator 1 (speaking into a handset) "Yes, we have a problem upstairs, we need a cleaner... some kind of stain... we don't know... it could be chocolate... it could be something worse... about two minutes ago... I don't know how to describe it... it's been smeared... there's a build-up in some areas, less in others. OK... OK... over and out."

With that she started laughing uncontrollably, which started her colleague off as well. On the other side of the gallery, I imagined, someone was stealing priceless art unobserved, the whole thing part of their fiendish plan.

Crane Train

Trapped on a motionless train somewhere in the north-east of England, I became aware of a voice behind me that sounded tense to the point of insanity. I turned to see a man who resembled a wildly overstimulated version of TV geographer Nicholas Crane unloading his woes on an elderly couple across the aisle.

Man "I mean the Victorians were going faster than this! Stevenson's rocket would be coming down here at, I won't say a hundred miles per hour – ninety though, at least!"

Old woman "And now you've got all those other stations on the way."

Man (calming himself for a moment) "It's a strange world."

Old woman "Yes it is."

Man (melting back into a frenzy) "You've got the TGV in France, the bullet train in Japan, why do we put up with it? Why?"

Old woman (realizing she no longer wanted to talk to him) "Mmm."

Man (regardless) "My favourite system is the Swiss network."

Old woman (willing him to cease) "Mmm."

Old man "I think we're almost in Newcastle."

Man (irate) "This is Gosforth!"

Old man (to his wife) "We'll get a cab from the station."

Man (uninvited) "Well, be advised. The centre of Newcastle is a no-go area. You can't take a car anywhere near it!"

He picked up his bags and leant over his victims. "Of course, my mother whizzes round the centre at eighty-two. She's a brave old soul." The implication being that his mother was a better class of pensioner altogether. And with that he dragged his bags towards the exit.

Old man (loudly, so as to disassociate himself from him) "Well I'm glad he's gone."

Audibly, the rest of the carriage exhaled in agreement.

Garage

On a night so cold one would only choose to leave the house if it were absolutely necessary, I found myself queuing to buy cigarettes in a petrol station behind a man whose errand was so bizarre that he must either have been a practising surrealist or mentally ill. He was holding a two-litre bottle of soft drink, a small amount of which had already been consumed.

Cashier "You want to buy that? That's all? No petrol?"

Man "I already bought it. I want to bring it back."

Cashier "What?"

Man (trying to force the bottle through the security hatch) "Look!"

Cashier "No! Stop that."

Man (grasping the futility of his action and giving up) "I've got the receipt."

Cashier (sensing a way out) "You must speak with my colleague."

With that he directed him to the other window, from where I was able to make out the following dialogue.

Cashier 2 "When did you buy this?"

Man (brandishing his receipt in one hand and his bottle in the other in a menacing way) "16th of December." (two weeks before) "I don't want it. I've got the receipt."

Cashier (struggling to hear through the security glass and probably not believing what he could make out) "Eh? I don't understand."

Man (louder) "I don't want it!"

His apparent ignorance of the dynamics of modern consumerism was matched by the continued bafflement of the cashier. As I left, the man was pressing his receipt up against the glass as though that would explain everything. It had the makings of a long stand-off. For all I know they may still be there.

iPods

Eavesdropping in a metropolis the size of London can be a dangerous thing. For every piece of wit, wisdom and banter gleaned from the conversations of strangers, you will hear something that can ruin your day, your week and maybe your life. It was in the departure lounge at Heathrow Terminal 3 where the following horrifically contemporary interchange occurred between two young British women flying to America to buy iPods.

Woman 1 (in an unpleasant high-pitched tone) "Do you know where the Apple store is in Chicago?"

Woman 2 "I've seen a map on the Internet. I think it's quite near the hotel."

Woman 1 "Will you get an iPod or a mini iPod?"

Woman 2 "I'm not sure."

There was a brief pause, during which the two women fell silent and revelled in their own modernity.

Woman 1 "When you're in bed with David, can you sleep?"

Woman 2 "What do you mean?"

Woman 1 "I mean, can you sleep with someone else in the bed? When Jake stays over I can never get to sleep. I get up feeling more tired than when I went to bed. I just hate having someone that near me."

At this point I felt compelled to turn around and look at her. It was a wonder Jake came round at all.

Woman 2 "It was a bit like that when we moved in together, but I'm used to it now."

Woman 1 "I absolutely hate it."

Woman 2 (drifting off) "I like the mini ones best, I like the colours."

Library

Paying a visit to my local library, I was dismayed to discover that the atmosphere of sternly enforced silence that reigned there years ago had been replaced by a culture of free expression in which the librarians were making the loudest remarks of all.

Librarian 1 (musing over where to go for dinner) "I dunno what I fancy. What's that place you're always on about, the one up the road?"

Librarian 2 (as though he were yelling at the deaf) "Oh it's blinding! The Duke of Kent's been in there – they've got a picture. I have the chicken. It's a good bit of breast, not like some of the rubbish you see. If you go in there and just have a starter, then it's not worth it, it doesn't add up. But the set deals are all right!"

Librarian 3 (anxious not be left out) "I had a biriani, a sizzler. You should have seen it."

Librarian 1 (sceptically) "Everywhere's shut though. Is it a Jewish holiday?"

Librarian 3 "Look in the calendar."

Librarian 1 "I will."

Librarian 2 "I been drinking a bit of that green tea lately."

Librarian 3 " You wanna be careful with that."

Librarian 2 "How so?"

Librarian 3 "There can be side effects if you don't know what you're doing. It's the Chinese who really know how to use it."

Librarian 1 "No. No Jewish holiday. But it is almost Burns Night."

Librarian 2 "What's that then? I don't like the sound of that."

I gave up on my reading there and then, having witnessed all too clearly that no matter how close you are to printed wisdom, there's no guarantee it will ever make you wise.

Lottery

Late on a Wednesday afternoon I found my attempts to buy an evening paper obstructed by a young woman whose desperation to win the midweek euro lottery had brought the local newsagents to a complete standstill. She appeared as excited about buying a ticket as you might expect someone to be about handing in a winning one. Two hapless cashiers struggled to assist her as her boyfriend stood by self-consciously.

Woman (with maniacal enthusiasm) "Two lucky dips! Two lucky dips!"

Newsagent 1 (fumbling with change and peering through thick glasses at her ticket) "You give me five pounds, yes?"

Woman "It's eighty million something, yeah?"

Newsagent 1 "You give me five pounds, two lucky dips and two numbers. You want more numbers?"

Woman (seemingly overwhelmed at the scale of her imminent victory) "I can't decide." To her boyfriend: "Choose some numbers! Think of some numbers!"

Boyfriend (staring blankly at confectionery) "I dunno babe."

Woman (to Newsagent 1) "What ones have I had?" He began to read them back to her at an agonizingly slow speed. By this time I had managed to assemble the correct change for my own purchase and was about to place it in front of the till, thus enabling me to escape. Newsagent 2 waved his hand at me in a gesture that indicated such a thing would be tantamount to theft, and I must wait to have my purchase officially scanned.

Woman "Oh, help me out, I can't think of no more numbers!"

Boyfriend (reluctantly) "One."

Woman "You can't have 'one'. Nobody has 'one'. You ain't getting any of this!" She waved the ticket at him in disdain. It was then that Newsagent 2's commercial instincts got the better of him and he reached out, took my money and nodded towards the door as if to say "Get out, go while you still can".

Wintour Wired Jaw

Some conversations are a struggle for superiority – conversations about illness especially so. In a London hotel dining room two late-middle-aged American women sat down to dinner with the clear intention of outdoing one another's recent adventures in the arena of the unwell.

Woman 1 "I don't know when middle age starts, thirty-five, forty-five? I say it's when you need glasses. I got mine when I was fifty-four."

Woman 2 "That's tremendous."

Woman 1 "Anyway, she was in the ER with this 'stomach ache', as she calls it. It turns out to be gall-stones BLOCKING HER BILE DUCT!"

This was said at such volume that I was compelled to look at her. She looked like a negative of Anna Wintour.

Woman 1 "Then she gets septemia."

Woman 2 "Septicaemia?"

Woman 1 "Yes. They had her on the wrong medication.

They were sending her to sleep. She's eighty-eight and they didn't know if her liver was bleeding or not."

Some food arrived, but not enough to keep them distracted.

Woman 2 (edging towards normality) "Oh this is delightful, it's like San Francisco!"

Woman 1 (having none of it) "And that wasn't the plan! Anyway, my sister went in and the nurse was sat there reading a magazine, while *she* was throwing up. They got there just in time, saved her life."

Woman 2 (not to be outdone) "Unbelievable. You know my mother has no bladder? Now they tell me she has suspect cells. And you know I broke my arm right at the very top – there was blood everywhere – and they wired my jaw shut…"

Whoever unwired it had a lot to answer for.

Industrial Action

Mid-afternoon inside a branch of a multinational fast-food concern, and a gang of workmen in fluorescent jackets listened intently as their foreman lobbied on their behalf over the phone.

Foreman "Well we've been kicked off site, that's the long and short of it… the ball's in their court now… we're all here doing absolutely nothing… from what they're saying we might have to go back in and finish it at night."

Workman 1 (shaking his head at the guy on the phone, who then covered the mouthpiece to enable the subsequent discussion) "Fuck that, I ain't doing it at night, and neither are this lot. It's too many hours pissing about and it's unsafe. Anyway look at him," (he gestured at one of his colleagues) "he misses his mother."

Workman 2 (in a comical Italian-style accent) "I miss-a my Mamma!"

Workman 1 (angrily) "Shaddup and finish your milk-shake! Anyway, I don't wanna miss the Argentina game."

Foreman (nodding in a fatalistic fashion) "I'll talk him into it. We'll do it tomorrow." He spoke into the phone again. "Look, there's nothing anyone here can do about it. It's the noise factor, that's what they told me. They walked in, shut us down and that was that. If we come back tonight, if they even *let* us come back tonight, who's to say it won't be the same story? I can understand you're not happy, you're not the only one. How do you think we feel? Well, you put the call in and we'll come back tomorrow – OK then. Fantastic."

He hung up the phone with a satisfied look, and the others, who were all eating, raised their unfinished burgers towards their saviour in a form of silent salute.

Knife Mum

While the influx of tourists into major cities in the summertime may be culturally enlightening for all concerned, from an eavesdropping point of view their banter can be immensely disappointing. All the gestures and intonations of fascinating conversation are present, but for the monolingual aural parasite their debates are pure frustration. So, on a long bus journey, when a pair of seats vacated by a pair of Japanese girls were taken by a mother and son in mid-argument, it seemed like divine intervention, even if it did sound like hell.

Mother (with theatrical anger) "I ain't going down for you boy! You better find that ticket. If the police storm this bus you're in trouble – it's a £20 fine now."

Son (indicating poster about fines) "No Mum, that's next month."

Mother "Whatever!"

The boy, evidently preparing to go on a camping trip of some sort, produced a cutlery set designed for outdoor living from a shopping bag and began to examine it.

Mother (almost gleefully) "Put that knife away! If the police find you with that, it's a weapon. They could do you!"

Whether these persistent references to the police in situations unlikely to merit their intervention was a radical new parenting technique or a reflex born from a lifetime of bitter experience, who could say? Wisely, the boy remained indifferent to his mother's legal hysteria.

Son (looking at knife forlornly) "It ain't even sharp."

Mother (turning to a newspaper but sticking to her theme) "Jacko's going down for getting them kids drunk, I reckon!"

But the boy just stared out the window, counting the minutes till his camping trip began.

Museum Flirtation Failure

In the cafeteria of a large museum an older man and a younger woman talked over the merits of the BBC's *Planet Earth*.

Woman (with genuine revulsion) "I thought it was disgusting. What kind of a place is that? That big pile of poo, all covered in cockroaches…"

Man (wincing slightly) "Yes, but the rock formations…"

Woman (undeterred) "And I saw the other one, I can't imagine spending all that time waiting for a fish to turn up."

Man (almost desperate) "But the caves! You must have seen the end of that episode, the rock formations were tremendous!"

Woman "Yeah."

Man (hopeful) "I've – er – I've been in two caves. I actually swam in one of them. The way in was tiny, you really had to steel yourself, it had a very high salt content, so it was freezing."

Woman "Where's that then?"

Man "In Bermuda – they only discovered it recently. Some kid lost his cricket ball down a hole and they found a whole network…"

Woman (defiantly) "I'm too claustrophobic."

Man (as though he was seriously about to take her there) "There is an easier way in."

Woman (uninterested) "I've got a bad knee. I was bad enough in that church spire we went up."

Man "You're lucky you didn't go up all the way: it became very narrow."

Woman "I don't care if the place was only open once a century, I wouldn't go again. I liked those paintings though, they use a lot of artistic licence."

Man (resigning himself to the fact that his *Educating Rita* fantasies had come to nothing) "Yes. Yes they do."

Nana Nanoo

A hot early afternoon in a pub garden, and the relative seclusion enjoyed by myself and its only other occupant – a woman reading a book – was shattered by another woman who sat down and commenced talking to her child over the phone.

Phone woman "Oh, I'm *so* glad everything's all right… yes… yes, Momma loves you… yes." At this point she put her mobile on speakerphone and broadcast both sides of the conversation.

Phone woman "Have you been swimming?"

Child's voice (weakly) "Yes."

Phone woman "Did you go out of your depth?"

Child "Yes."

Phone woman "Were you with Nana?"

Child "Yes."

Phone woman "And Nanoo?"

Child "Yes."

What kind of person encourages a child to call their Granddad "Nanoo", I wondered? There was no clear reason why she had switched to speakerphone either. I thought she might have been friends with book woman, but this wasn't the case. And then an actual friend of book woman arrived and started looking at phone woman slightly askance.

Book woman (to her friend) "I been reading this book – it's really interesting, it's about Afghanistan."

Friend "Don't talk to me about books, I've got about five at home that I haven't read yet."

Phone woman (off speakerphone now, but still at high volume) "I LOVE YOU!"

Book woman (undeterred) "It used to be all kings and that, it's gone from one extreme to another – there's a great line in it. It says the worst thing you can do in life is to be a liar – or is it a thief? Either way it's an amazing account of…"

Phone woman "I LOVE YOU!"

Book woman (giving up and picking up a menu) "Ooh, anyway, bring on the barbecue."

Phone woman "I LOVE YOU MORE!" And with that she hung up, and left Nana and Nanoo to get on with it.

Newt Planner

Boarding an intercity train, I was walking towards a seat directly behind an elderly man in a three-piece suit. He smiled politely as I passed him, and I thought, "There's a bloke who won't be talking on his phone the whole way." It was a huge mistake. No sooner had the train left the station than he embarked on a business deal that went on for the best part of an hour.

Man (perfectly spoken but incredibly loud) "He's a very rich man, my client. Based in Australia. I have to tell you that he won't sell unless it's the top offer. Otherwise it would have gone a long time ago... It would have to be a special purchase... It's four acres, of which you can build on three. There has to be a buffer between the residential and the industrial."

But just as the whole carriage was praying for a quick sale, a new factor entered the equation.

Man (forcefully) "There are crested newts! You mustn't disturb them. It's a registered site."

The buyer rang off and called back.

Man "He won't take less than eight hundred and twenty-five."

Over the next half an hour the conversation stopped and resumed as the signal permitted. The man's descriptions blended into a collage of real-estate terms.

Man "It's twenty minutes from the motorway... no more than six to eight weeks... principal planning officer... Greenfield site... you must respect the residential... lose half an acre... access is via a hammerhead road."

Hammerhead road? You could instantly visualize it, but whoever heard it called that? There's a reason rich people are rich, I thought. They have their own language. But then he came down to earth suddenly.

Man (seductively) "If it's quick I'll take less."

Aha, I thought. You're just like everyone else.

Crook Brooks

In a busy pub I was jammed on to a table with two men who were struggling to make themselves heard above the sound of the adjacent jukebox. It transpired that their failure to comprehend one another was due as much to drunkenness as decibel level, and I found myself conscripted into their debate as an interpreter.

Man 1 (shouting above Robbie Williams' version of 'Mr Bojangles') "I hate Garth Crooks!"

Man 2 (the drunker of the pair, persistently rolling a cigarette) "Eh?"

Man 1 (louder) "I said I hate Garth Crooks, off *Match of the Day*!"

Man 2 "Who's he on about?"

Me "He said he hates Garth Crooks."

Man 2 "Eh?"

Me "Garth Crooks… used to play for Tottenham?"

Man 2 "Oh I hate country and western!"

Man 1 (to Man 2, having heard just enough to confuse things even further) "What are you talking about?"

Man 2 (almost screaming) "I SAID, I DON'T LIKE COUNTRY AND WESTERN!"

Me (trying to defuse matters) "He thinks you said Garth Brooks, not Garth Crooks."

Man 1 "Who the fuck is Garth Brooks?"

Me (at both of them, with actions) "Garth Brooks is a country-and-western singer, Garth Crooks does the football on BBC 1"

Man 2 (uninterested) "Since Elvis, most American music's gone downhill."

Me (to Man 1) "I don't think he knows what you're talking about."

Man 1 "I know he doesn't, he's an idiot. You don't wanna waste your time talking to him."

Man 2 "I heard that!"

Man 1 "Good. I meant it!"

Me "I'm going to the toilet."

I got up, pushed into the crowd and never came back.

Oz Debt

Working my way through a samosa outside a takeaway on a Sunday afternoon, my attention was taken by someone shouting loudly in an Australian accent.

Man "I haven't forgotten that I owe you fifteen hundred dollars, absolutely no way... you can depend on that!"

I looked up to see a young man dressed in tight black clothing, yelling into a mobile while marching in circles and gesticulating wildly, as though he were part of a performance-art piece called 'Australian Goth/Muso on Mobile Phone'.

Man "I'm homeless, I'm jobless, I'm skint... yeah, I'm sorry but unless something happens now, quick sticks, I don't know what I'm gonna do. Oh listen though, fuck me!"

He repeated the expletive as if on the brink of a life-changing revelation.

Man "Fuck – me. Have I got some tunes for you? You wanna hear 'em. I'm gonna come back over there at

Christmas and, whoah, are we gonna get one hell of a rave going in that front room! You still got that sound system set up in there? That's what I'm talking about mate. Fucking good times!"

He stopped circling for a moment and started kicking at a wire fence.

Man "I can tell you're pissed about the money, Mark. I can sense that. We're gonna get all that squared up just as soon as we can. How is everyone over there anyway? Pretty much the same old scene, eh? Hey, no… listen, I am on the case with that money."

It was at this point he started making feedback-type noises with his mouth.

Man "I'm losing you Mark."

He held the phone away from him.

Man "Mate, I'm losing you."

He hung up quite deliberately and looked at me as if to say "What are you going to do about it?" I did my best to look back at him, as if to say "Absolutely nothing, mate. Your excuses are your own."

Phone Bust

A man walked back into a pub looking at his mobile phone as if whatever grim news he'd just heard was actually the fault of the handset. He slammed it on the table and sat back down with his friend.

Man 1 (exasperated) "She knows, man."

Man 2 (blasé) "I don't know why you answer it."

Man 1 (shaking his head) " She's *so* angry."

Man 2 (assuming the James Bolam role from *The Likely Lads*) "Your problem is that you're not naturally deceitful. You're not a good liar. She should be grateful for that. You're an honest bloke."

Man 1 (too distressed even to pick up his pint) "Hmmn."

Man 2 "You sound guilty, even when there's nothing wrong."

Man 1 (seizing his phone and waving it about) "She gets the numbers out of my phone!"

Man 2 (with growing indignation) "She goes through your phone! That's against the rules. She's looking for trouble, and now she's found it."

Man 1 (with resigned honesty) "But the numbers were in there, you know. She was right. I did do it."

Man 2 (sensing he was about to be abandoned and getting desperate) "Yeah, but even so. Now everyone's unhappy. It's not gonna make any difference when you get home."

Man 1 "I better go home."

Man 2 (evidently thinking of himself) "Well now she's ruined everyone's day."

Man 1 (rising to leave) "Look, I didn't say I was with you."

Man 2 "Thank fuck for that."

Man 1 "I'll see you later."

Man 2 "Yeah."

Then he tipped his friend's pint into his own glass and scowled.

Plane Woman

Waiting to get off a plane at Heathrow in one of those un-pleasant interludes between the seat-belt sign going off and the doors opening and anyone actually going anywhere, I became aware of the woman across the aisle from me interrogating a steward in a high-handed manner.

Woman (as though addressing an errant member of domestic staff in the nineteenth century) "I do not wish to leave the airport, I am merely transferring. Ideally I shall be in Vancouver by tomorrow morning. That is my final destination. The question which I am asking you is whether it is necessary for me to display my passport and so forth within the terminal. I am in transit. Do you understand?"

Steward (evidently accustomed to this level of enquiry) "Well madam, if your bags were checked through, then you can go to the transit—"

Woman (interrupting) "I suspected as much. I will be needing some money too. Is there a machine in this area?"

Steward "Yes, when you come into the terminal—"

Woman "What kind of machine is it? Can I use it?"

Steward "I'm not sure, I think it's a Barclays."

Woman "Splendid, I am with Barclays. Are you with Barclays?"

Steward (somewhat baffled) "Er, no. I'm with one of the other banks, but—"

Woman (reaching for a piece of vernacular quite at odds with her age and demeanour) "Whatever!"

Steward "Right, so are you happy then?"

Woman "As far as I am concerned, the sooner I and my bags arrive in Vancouver, the happier I shall be."

The steward looked as though he was in complete agreement, then the doors opened and she waltzed away to become somebody else's problem.

Plumber

A plumber came round the house recently and, after he'd fixed the boiler and given me a refresher course in the rudiments of maintaining your own central-heating system, I thought I'd try and make some small talk.

Me "So, are you busy at the moment?"

Plumber "Busy? I've had a busy couple of months!"

Me "That's good."

Plumber "Is it? Everything's gone mad since I had me eyes done."

Me "How do you mean?"

Plumber "I used to wear glasses, right? Well I've gone in and had that operation so I don't need 'em no more, and that's when it started. A week after I come out of hospital, I'm in the pub and I've punched this bloke…"

Me "What for?"

Plumber "Can't remember. But someone's rugby-tackled me and I've gone over and broke me arm. So I'm out of action. So I'm stuck at home all day, start feeling a bit sick, headaches, coughing up blood, back down the hospital, and I've got pneumonia! They've kept me in – tubes all over the place. Get out of there, I'm all depressed, start drinking again, had an argument with the missus and I threw a saucepan at her. Didn't mean to hit her, and it didn't go anywhere near her, so I've got to bed, but she's phoned the Old Bill! Next thing I know there's four coppers standing over the bed going, 'You're coming with us.' I said you must be joking. They took me away, and they only didn't put me in handcuffs cos I still had the broken arm."

Me "Blimey."

Plumber "And all this since I had the eyes done."

Me "You think it's connected?"

Plumber "Course it is. I've messed about with the laws of nature, and this is nature having a go back at me!"

Swiss Ball

Hanging around outside a pub waiting for someone to buy me a drink, I found myself next to two men, one of whom was in the middle of an extraordinary confession. He looked like a coil of barely repressed violence, masked somewhat by an unconvincing beard. His associate was covered in elaborate tattoos and was deriving considerable pleasure from his friend's predicament.

Man 1 "Anyway, I'd been winding Tom up about having one of those exercise balls in his flat, saying they were a bit, you know…"

Man 2 "Gay?"

Man 1. "Yeah. Then the physio tells me I've gotta get one! So I started using one at the gym, and this proper Herbert on the weight machine next to me goes, 'Why don't you take your ball and fuck off somewhere else?'"

Man 2 "You didn't stand for that?"

Man 1 "No. I squared up to him. They had to separate us in the end."

Man 2 "What exactly were you doing?"

Man 1 "I had to stand on this trampette and bounce the ball against the wall."

Man 2 (laughing) "I can't believe you said 'trampette'."

Man 1 "What do you mean?"

Man 2 "Never mind the ball, you don't wanna go around saying 'trampette' – you could have said 'small trampoline'."

Man 1 "Anyway, I'm banned now. So I had to go and get one of these balls from the shop. I took it home, but I didn't have a pump, so I sat on the sofa and blew it up with my mouth. It never seemed to get full enough, so in the end I give it all I had and the fucking thing blew up in my face!"

Man 2 (almost hysterical) "No!"

Man 1 "Yeah. So I took it back and there's these two shop assistants openly mocking me, going, 'It blew up in your face, bruv?' Pissing themselves."

Man 2 "So what did you do?"

Man 1 "Well I had to put up with it didn't I? I needed the refund."

Public Nuisance

It was that time of the evening when the clientele of pubs are changing shifts between drinkers who have turned up straight from work and are about to head for home and the arrival of those who will be around till closing time. As a member of the latter party, I approached the bar to find myself confronted by a man who, in terms of his own intoxication, was clearly anxious to put in a bit of overtime. He was short, and his tie was already sliding away from his neck. As his colleagues' body language spoke of imminent departure, he wedged himself closer to the optics, waved money at the bar staff and told everyone what he thought of everything.

Man "I mean, he's a personal friend of mine, a great number two, and I think he'd say this himself – he's not a natural leader. He's quite exuberant with clients, you know what I'm saying? Put him in front of a client – they'll like him. Put him on a job and ask him to put a bid analysis together, no problem. He's a personal friend of mine, I went to his wedding."

Colleague "What happened with you and John? I heard you fell out with him…"

Man (defiantly) "There was no fall-out! Those guys just wouldn't give any equity away."

I moved away, and over the next hour so did everyone he was with. By eleven o'clock he could barely stand and was talking into his mobile, trying to meet up with someone for a curry, when he asked the landlady for advice on where to go.

Man (loudly into his phone) "Apparently, there's a restaurant round the corner called 'Twat'!"

He looked round the pub as though expecting the crowd to collapse with laughter. But he had completely miscalculated and people just stared at him. He lowered his voice, picked up his jacket and slunk off into the night in pursuit of nutrition and a new audience.

Shot in the Face

On top of a bus I was overwhelmed by a series of exchanges between a group of young people who were doing that thing you do sometimes – discussing matters of no importance as though they were the most important things in the world. What was interesting about it was that, although many of their outbursts appeared independent from one another, at the same time they seemed linked to the consciousness of the whole, like neural flashes in a collective brain.

Girl 1 (as if accusing someone of murder) "I can't believe it – Christmas is, like, a month away or something, and you lot are already getting vexed! I don't get excited until two days beforehand, maximum."

Girl 2 "I'm getting one of them Morgan dresses, like a cocktail dress."

All girls together (with sarcastic affection) "Ooh."

Girl 1 "What's the song on that advert? It's pissing me off!"

Remaining girls (singing along to music emanating from a phone) "You've got to show me love…"

Boy 1 "Can I tell you something? Have you been to Hampstead Heath? That is one sick lido!"

Boy 2 "Gays go moonlighting there though, innit?"

Girl 2 "Ugh, Janet Jackson, she is so butters."

Girl 3 (answering her phone) "What you phonin' me for? I was listening to a song."

Boy 1 "Have you ever had food in court?"

Boy 2 "In Catford nick they will bring you a Mc-Donald's if you ask them, I'm serious."

Boy 1 "You know that guy from school who was shot in the face?"

Boy 2 "Yeah."

Boy 1 "Well he's having a party."

Boy 2 "If we go we can't start no beef."

Boy 1 "I wouldn't start no beef anyway."

With that the bus pulled up by a famous theatre school and they all piled inside. Blimey, I thought, there goes the future cast of *The Bill*.

Sonic Chameleon

On a warm late-summer lunchtime break, I found myself gnawing at a sandwich in a public park, just across from a dynamic young office type going out of his way to impress his female underling with tales of his own greatness.

Man "If I spend a couple of weeks in Saudi, I've got a Saudi accent before you know it. If I'm here much longer, I'll sound like you, some sort of cockney. If I'm working out of the Sydney office, then forget about it, you'd think I was Australian. I just blend in and assume people's characteristics. I can't help it!"

Woman (sucking a drink up through a straw indifferently) "S'at right?"

Man "Totally. I'm a kind of sonic chameleon. You know what a chameleon is?"

Woman "Like an insect."

Man "Well, it changes colour in order to survive. It blends in."

Woman "Right."

Man (ominously) "It blends in so that it can survive. And it survives so that it can breed."

The woman slurped up the last of her drink and gazed into space.

Man (changing his angle) "The thing about me is I don't want to make the bloody software, I just want to design it, you know? I'm about taking this thing up a gear, I'm sick of how some of what we do in the industry can be offensive to other cultures. And I'm especially sick of how offensive some of it is to women."

Woman (without looking at him) "I'm going back to work now."

Man "I'll come with you."

Woman "Right."

Touts

It was a scene familiar to any gig-goer. In the underpass leading to a famous rock-'n'-roll venue, touts announced their intention to "buy or sell" tickets for the evening's sold-out show. In what would develop into an epic culture clash as well as a display of championship-level swearing, a naive youngster enquired as to the possibility of making a deal.

Tout (already angry) "'Ow much money yer got?"

Man (rattled, and trying to put his wallet back in his pocket) "Well, I – er – I don't know – that depends – how much are they?"

Tout (with added impatience) "Owmanygerwant?"

Man "Well, three, I think, but…"

Tout (reaching towards him and beckoning for cash whilst theatrically looking about for "the law") "'Undredandtwennypahnd!"

Man (recoiling) "Are the seats together?"

Tout (his face changing colour in a manner ordinarily confined to marine life) "No they fuckin' well ain't!"

Man (growing paler in vivid contrast to his adversary) "Well to be honest I was hoping for three together."

Tout "Well you ain't gonna find none. It's me or nothing, so pay up or fuck off out of it."

Man (backing off) "To be honest, I think I'll try my luck elsewhere."

Tout "Yeah? Well fuck your luck. Fuck off to fucking elsewhere, you fucking arsehole!"

Man (evidently determined to leave the encounter with no credibility at all) "I'm sorry."

Tout (not even looking at him) "Fuck off!"

Bit unnecessary, I thought as I trudged towards the venue. Then I got inside, and it was open seating anyway.

Train Boy

On an overcrowded train from Manchester to London, I watched with selfish dismay as the seats around me were taken up by a woman with three young children, one of whom was only weeks old, the eldest a boy of around five. The boy was in a state of wild excitement that he succeeded in sustaining for the full three-hour journey. Before the train had even started moving, he was barking at his mother for information.

Boy "Where are we going?"

Mum "London."

Boy (noticing that the woman in the seat in front also had a very young child) "Mum, Mum! There's a baby here. Do you think the baby would like to see our baby?"

Mum "The babies are asleep."

Boy "Are we still in Manchester?"

Mum "Yes."

Boy "Where are we going?"

Mum "London."

Boy "Can I have an apple?"

Mum "Here."

Boy (so loudly that he woke both babies, who started crying) "Not that one!"

Mum "Just eat it."

Boy "I like salt…What's vinegar?"

Mum "I use it in the kitchen."

Boy "Can you show me when we get home?"

Mum "Yes."

Boy "How many seconds will that be?"

Mum "Lots."

Boy "Will it be as many as 100,000?"

Mum "Yes."

Boy "Where are we?"

Mum "Between London and Manchester."

Boy "Are we in summer? Why is the sun out?"

Mum "This is autumn."

Boy "Why is orange called *orange*? Is it because of the fruit?"

Mum "Yes."

Boy (reading the label on a packet of sweets) "Am I a young child?"

Mum "Yes."

Boy (alarmed) "Then I could choke on one of these!"

I couldn't help wishing he had done.

Lift Yank

Two huge lifts arrived simultaneously in front of a crowd of underground commuters to take them up and out of the station. It took less than a second for me to realize I had got into the wrong one. The man wedged immediately to the left of me, who I had assumed to be an adult, was in fact an American high-school student with an unusually dense beard. Before the doors had even closed he started shouting.

Beard boy "Hey, hey! What do you figure the time is back home?"

Fellow student (female, across the lift) "I dunno, it's like six hours back so…"

Another student (all eager) "It's noon."

Beard boy "Why don't we like not eat till the others are eating, I mean like only eat in the same time zone?"

Other students "Yeah, right!"

Teacher (pinned up against the far side of the lift) "We've reservations at six-thirty, you guys do what you want – but I tell you this, I am eating tonight."

Beard boy (believing he had struck a rich comic vein) "Hey, like you're in charge of student-body integration, but I don't see you doing a whole lot of integrating. You should eat when we wanna eat, right?"

Other student "Hur hur, yeah."

Beard boy "Yeah, and like I think we should all be sleeping in the same room, the way things are is like the dumbest thing. We should be more, like, integrated – and that is down to you dude."

Teacher (as though suddenly sensing the collective will of the other passengers) "Shut up, Darrell."

"Yeah, Darrell. Shut up. Shut up and shave," I had to stop myself from saying.

Trouble with the Normal

Two men in a pub, one in his thirties and the other in his sixties, sat next to each other without speaking. Coincidentally, they removed their jackets at the same moment, and this was all the excuse the older man needed to strike up a conversation with his neighbour.

Man 1 "Warm in here, innit?"

Man 2 (instantly perturbed at the thought of speaking to a stranger) "Yes it is a bit."

Man 1 (nodding towards the barmaid) "I think I'm in love!"

Man 2 (unsure how to bring such a dialogue to an end) "Good for you."

Man 1 (more than willing, possibly psychologically compelled to switch topics, turned towards the television) "Watching the football?"

Man 2 "No."

Man 1 (increasingly less worried about getting a response) "Shearer's had a punch-up, taken a knock. I don't get Sky, I have enough trouble with the normal.

Some bastard come round me house the other day asking for a TV whatsit – I've only been there three fucking days so I've told him where to stick it. They've got the whole block marked out I reckon, no one there's got any money."

The younger man was now faking an interest in football to avoid his new friend's gaze. But his new friend didn't care.

Man 1 "Voting's the same – had a letter from them wanting two grand if you don't write back! Two grand! I ain't filling out no fucking forms for nothing. Though I did in the end. Who am I gonna vote for? I ain't even got no furniture. I'm painting a fella's wall round the corner and he's gonna give me his sofa, which is worth a grand."

Man 2 "I'm going to the toilet."

Man 1 (turning to the barmaid) "What's your name then?"

Pub Food

A young man and a couple in a pub, who had taken the audacious move of bringing their own takeaway in with them, finished eating and proceeded to wind each other up in lieu of dessert.

Man 1 (turning to his friend's spouse) "How are you? You're looking all right. Not too pale. Cos you haven't seen him for a while innit. He's a handful, isn't he? Bit of a worry."

Woman (quietly laughing) "After about twelve pints."

Man 1 (with exaggerated alarm) "Twelve pints? He's *always* a problem, even people who don't know him – people who just *observe* him – find him hard work."

Man 2 (with a mixture of mirth and admonishment, whilst reclining backwards over a pool table) "Easy!"

Man 1 "All I'm saying is it's miraculous how well she looks – and I ask myself what is the source of this miracle? And it's got to be that she hasn't seen you for a couple of weeks."

Man 2 "Yeah, yeah."

Man 1 (gladly raising the stakes) "I bet you haven't even been crying lately."

Woman (indignant) "When was I crying?"

Man 1 "In here two weeks ago, everyone saw you."

Woman (clearly no stranger to this kind of probing dialogue) "When are you gonna get a proper girlfriend?"

Man 1 (with theatrical regret) "I haven't been in love since I was eighteen. I imagine it would be quite difficult for me to find love now."

Man 2 (with great conviction) "Love finds you."

Man 1 (aghast) "Eh?"

Man 2 "Love finds you, innit."

Man 1 (utterly unconvinced and a little annoyed) "Get a grip on yourself." And with that he marched off defiantly towards the toilet.

God Loves…

Another shop, another outburst of spontaneous conversational insanity. This time I was in a newsagent's, buying a magazine, when I became conscious of a rising hullabaloo emanating from the podium where people fill in their lottery tickets. I turned to see a man there I recognized as a notorious local traffic-botherer and behavioural innovator. He is in his fifties and favours a black bandanna.

Man (to no one in particular, but very loudly) "Numbers! Bastard! You'll never win you know? Never win. But I tell you this, God loves a tryer."

He finished his ticket and approached the counter, where I was in the middle of my transaction. In addition to the shopkeeper, there was an old man, possibly his father, standing behind the counter with his eyes closed, and it was to him that the man now turned his attention.

Man "Do you speak English?"

Shopkeeper (stepping in on the older man's behalf) "He is sleeping."

The old man just kept his eyes shut and smiled, as though he were being fellated in a parallel universe.

Man "Well he wants to wake up. It's a quarter past one."

Again, the old man did nothing.

Man (slamming his ticket down on the counter) "You know who wins the lottery? Paedophiles win the lottery!"

Shopkeeper (processing the ticket) "Good luck, sir."

Man "What do you mean? Are you saying I'm a paedophile? Is that what you're saying?"

Shopkeeper (immune to such behaviour through experience) "Here, take your ticket sir."

Man (backing out of the shop) "If you believe in justice you're a bloody fool!"

And then he was out of the door, with an air of purpose that suggested there was traffic out there that wasn't going to yell at itself.

Paint Points

Eating pizza in a restaurant at lunchtime, I caught wind of two men on the table behind me discussing the perils of interior design.

Man 1 "She showed me all the paints and asked me which one I liked. I said I didn't mind – that we'd get whatever she wanted."

Man 2 "How did that go down?"

Man 1 "Well she lost it, there and then. Starts saying I don't care, I don't take enough of interest, all that number."

Man 2 "Yeah, they resent all that. You say 'you decide', and it's like a red rag."

Man 1 "So I've gone the other way – if you want my opinion you can have it, you know what I'm saying?"

Man 2 "I hear you."

Man 1 "So I've looked at 'em all and said what I like, and now, of course, we can't agree: she's chosen different ones from me, so I really throw myself into it. There's forty-eight paints on the chart right? And there's six that we like between us. So I said to her we'll have six points each to give to our favourite paints – distribute them any way we like – and then the one with the most points is the colour we use."

Man 2 "Brilliant!"

Man 1 "Innit? But then I've gone a step further. I give all six of my points to the one I like and she's split all hers up into 1.5s like I knew she would. So I've won!"

Man 2 (laughing) "You've gone too far there!"

Man 1 "I know, and I could see she was upset, so I just said look, why don't you choose?"

Man 2 "That's fair. What colour did you end up with?"

Man 1 (proudly, through a mouthful of food) "Impala."

Sneeze

I could tell the woman sitting behind me on the train had a bad head cold, because she kept making all the sounds that go with that affliction, but the real giveaway was the fact that she kept calling people on her mobile and telling them she had a cold. "I'm on the train, I've got a cold," she kept saying. "I'll phone you later." The fourth time she did it, a conversation broke out.

Woman (nasally, like someone in an advert for cough sweets) "I tell you what, it's a weird place, they've got a Pizza Hut Express in the town centre. There's people walking round everywhere eating these tiny pizzas..." (with extra astonishment) "Yeah, tiny little pizzas! It's mental... I couldn't stay there another night in the end... she said she had work today – which is fair enough, cos she's got these nursing exams, so I was like, I'll leave you to it then – oh, hang on..."

She then let out an enormous sneeze containing sufficient moisture that I could feel particles of it condensing on my neck.

Woman "Ooh dear, that were a big one – anyway, then her boyfriend comes in and says, 'Do you wanna go to the Rhino?'… it's a club in town, and she was like 'Yeah', so I was a little bit offended like, but I couldn't say anything like, so I just packed my bags and got on the train. I'd only been there for a day, and now I'm on me way back! Oh…"

Then came the biggest sneeze yet, it made my hair move. I got up thinking I'd remonstrate with her, but when I turned round she was looking right at me – I lost my nerve and had to front it out by walking down the carriage and pretending to use the toilet.

Tube Mad

Years of bitter experience and basic human instinct teach you to steer clear of mass transit systems after closing time at weekends, but sometimes there's nothing else you can do. At the tail end of a journey already punctuated by the screams and cries of the Friday-night faithful, I boarded another tube train and encountered what initially appeared to be an everyday scene. A young though slightly feral man was making conversation with two women opposite.

Man "That's me. That's how I am. I'm friendly. I don't care. I say what I think."

The women were beaming at him with no nervousness at all. As the train reached the next station, he removed his cap in a theatrical way.

Man "Ladies, it has been my pleasure!" He kissed their hands, and they laughed and stood up and left. There had seemed to be such an easy intimacy that I was surprised to see that they were not travelling together. Two other young women immediately replaced them.

Man "All right ladies, I'm Brian. What do you do?"

Woman (surprisingly convivial) "I'm a nanny."

Man (at inappropriate volume) "ALL RIGHT NAN?!"

He shook their hands, yet they remained composed.

Man (removing his shirt to reveal his torso) "I don't need no looking after!" He began to do press-ups on the carriage floor. "Where you going?"

Woman (to my amazement) "Morden."

Man (finishing press-ups and sitting down) "All the way, me too!"

They all laughed. By now the train was at my station, and I moved nervously between them to leave. I considered passing them a note that said "Run while you can, he is insane". But I didn't have a pen and, for the moment at least, they didn't appear to have a problem.

The Water Margin

I was struggling to operate the water cooler in the entrance hall of a business centre when a courier walked in and approached the receptionist, a woman in her fifties with candy-floss hair who – it transpired – could have single-handedly paved the road to hell with just one of her good intentions.

Courier (removing his helmet) "Do you have any mail for us, a courier?"

Receptionist "No dear." (then suddenly looking up and noting the colour of his skin) "Actually yes, I have seen something. Er – it's for a Mr Akuja – would that be you dear?"

Courier "It's from Akuja, and yes, that's it."

Receptionist (handing over the package) "What part of the world are you originally from, dear?"

Courier "Nigeria."

Receptionist (excited) "Did you see that programme on TV last night, what was it called? *The Last Slave*. It was very good, very interesting, you know?"

Courier (unmoved) "I don't have a TV."

Receptionist (undeterred) "Don't you dear? It was great, very interesting. Did you know it wasn't just the white men who trafficked in slaves?"

Courier "I don't watch TV, I only listen to the radio."

Receptionist (pointing at TV screen, where they were talking about Senator Barack Obama) "Then you must have heard about that guy. Did you know that his great-great-grandfather had fifty slaves or something?"

Courier (leaving) "I've gotta go."

Receptionist (calling after him) "It's shocking though, isn't it?"

As he strode purposefully past, I clung fast to the water cooler, hoping that the sheer force of my own self-consciousness might somehow make me invisible.

Scots Wheel

In a bar in Edinburgh I popped out for a cigarette and found another smoker – very drunk – attempting to goad the pub's bouncer into a debate about Ferris wheels.

Drinker (gazing up at the illuminated wheel in front of him – a splendid sight by any conventional yardstick) "What's the point of it anyway – you're up again, down again. Life's hard enough already without spending it going round in a fuckin' wheel!"

The bouncer looked him up and down as though he were measuring him for a coffin, but said nothing.

Drinker (turning his full attention on the bouncer now) "There's too many of 'em anyway, I reckon. Since they stuck that thing up in London, everyone else thinks they have to have one. Fuckin' Manchester, York, Birmingham, this thing here… These are just the ones I've seen with me own eyes. There could be more, there probably is more. There's wheels everywhere, it's invasion of the fuckin'… Ferris thing, innit?"

Bouncer (effortlessly pitching a polite reply so it sounded like a death threat) "Is that right?"

Drinker (too wrapped up in his theory to pick up the warning signs, pointing at the bouncer as he spoke) "You been up there? I'm saying, have you been up there?"

The doorman just shook his head and kept his eyes on him while shifting his shoulders slightly as if preparing to make a move.

Drinker (trying to grab the doorman's arm) "Let's go up there now, me and you. I'm paying, come on…"

Bouncer (grabbing his arm, firmly) "I don't like heights."

Drinker (angrily) "I don't like the way you're holding my arm!"

Bouncer (bending the man's arm around) "You got a drink in there?"

Drinker (totally submissive suddenly) "Yes, sorry."

Bouncer "You wanna finish it?"

Drinker "Please."

Bouncer "Then get back inside and leave me the fuck alone."

The man went back inside. The doorman looked at me as if to say "Got anything to say about Ferris wheels?" I looked back as if to say "Not really, no".

Bagel Bike

In shops you visit regularly, you come to develop a sense of expectation about how they work, which way the queue goes, the protocols of service and so forth. When these patterns are disturbed, it can lead to a tangible feeling of resentment towards the perpetrators. It was precisely this parochial sense of fury that filled me when I entered a local bakery to find a man shouting and riding a small bicycle up and down the floor. He looked around fifty years old, with wild grey hair sprouting from under a flat cap and a face that suggested years of alcohol and outdoor living. James Blunt's 'You're Beautiful' was playing on the radio.

Bike man (circling somehow in such a confined space) "James Blunt! James Blunt! I'm a James Blunt!" He skidded to a halt at my feet and announced to no one in particular, "Rhyming slang, innit? James Blunt!" I could see where this was going and feigned interest in some éclairs.

Man at till (Evidently bike man's accomplice, same sort of age but carrying a huge rucksack and various other packages) "Are we having tea – do you want tea?"

Woman at till (losing patience with their antics and in a pronounced Russian accent) "How many teas? Large or small?"

Till man answered, and bike man pulled up next to him. Till man then produced a DVD from one of his bundles. It was Roman Polanski's *The Fearless Vampire Slayers*.

Bike man "Funny as fuck!"

Till man "Will you let us watch it?"

Bike man "Tonight? Yeah, why not."

I began to wonder at their domestic arrangements – bail hostel, halfway house, eccentric millionaires with a taste for European film and cheap buns, who knew? They left the shop with bike man clearing the way laughing, and his subordinate struggling with the teas. The disoriented customers and staff stayed frozen for a moment before order was restored, as James Blunt assured us of our beauty on the radio.

All Ears... Behind the Scenes

Dog Death
This actually happened to me on holiday, I ended up telling the story so often I thought I'd borrow it for the column. After we left, the dog – which lives in Canada – made a miraculous recovery, and at the time of writing is still alive.

Poirot
This was the Barcelona vs Arsenal game in May 2006. The bar in question is on Great Eastern Street in London.

Bank
NatWest bank, Shoreditch High Street, a living monument to inertia.

Kebab
The shop in question is located on the corner of Hackney Road and Kingsland Road. The staff have seen so much action that they've developed a kind of "thousand doner stare" which enables them to ignore a good deal of what comes their way. What was interesting about this was that the guy who came in initially seemed unreasonable and intimidating, but in the end he completely turned things around and left the guys in the shop looking like they were doing him a disservice by refusing to help him out.

Cider Women

This pair were quite remarkable, everything about the setting is true, including the brand of cider. It was the first off-peak service of the day from Southampton to Waterloo, packed, and as a consequence I ended up sharing a table with these two, who must have started drinking somewhere down the line in Dorset. We were together for over an hour. A lot more was said, but, believe me, this was the best of it.

Landmines

This was lunchtime on New Year's Eve 2006/7, the restaurant-canteen in Spitalfields market seemed to be full of people coming to terms with things they'd done the night before while bracing themselves to do it all over again.

Eastern Promise

This was at a house party near Alexandra Palace. The food was particularly good, so much so that people were concentrating more on what they were eating than who they were eating it with, which is how this particular conversation wound up being the focus of attention in a room full of strangers.

John Lewis

This was the first of many dispatches from the upper deck of the No. 8. It was early evening, spring into summer, and there was a sense of peculiar optimism in the air that one only seems to stumble across at that time of day and year, until this dude started leaping up and down in the front seat as though he were coordinating the Normandy landings.

Locker

Health club off Curtain Road, East London.

Respect Bus
Bus No. 55, eastbound, Old Street, March 2006.

Mercenary
This is the first part of the Spanish bar conversation, detailed on page 49.

Phone Panic
Franco's Café, Rivington Street, East London, 2006.

Rave Toilet
The place where this happened is just off the southern end of City Road in London, the difference between the two floors was quite astounding, they could have been existing in completely different decades with the toilets serving as a sort of portal between them. Very odd clientele too.

Cricket
This was the morning of the first day of the fourth test in August 2006, which was abandoned after allegations of "ball tampering". As well as the guys in this story, a once prominent Conservative MP was also sitting close by, and spent much of the day complaining about the Government's policy on terrorism. "This lot are running scared", he reckoned, whereas "under Margaret" things would have been very different.

Shoe Conkers
King's Cross Station, waiting for the Glasgow train to depart, November 2006. After this was published the woman in the story wrote to the Guardian. *She worked in an art gallery in Edinburgh and*

described the experience of seeing what she had assumed to be a private moment appearing in print as "really disconcerting". Often I find myself being quite disparaging about the people that I write about, but luckily I hadn't been so in this case. "We were hugely pleased to be thought well dressed", she explained. Because I was sitting just behind her and able to make clear notes, I knew it was a faithful reproduction of what they had said to each other, and she was kind enough to clarify things further. Her friend, she explained, was "a gay chap… hence the familiarity, not intimacy". She also pointed out that the baby in question was a girl – her brother's daughter – and not a boy.

Snake Builder
This was told to me by a friend who heard it while he was having breakfast one day in a café on Cambridge Heath Road, Hackney. He was very specific about the accents, as well as key dialogue points, like the type of snake and the ferocity of its bite relative to that of a hamster.

Social Work
Outside The Coach & Horses, Greek Street, Soho, summer 2005.

Celery Boy
This is a story from a friend of mine who once worked in a butcher's in Nuneaton. I threw in the lunchtime detail to give it some context.

Tall Colleague
Franco's Café, Rivington Street, East London. I've been back there since, hoping the tall man might show himself, but he hasn't yet.

This was one of the first conversations I made a note of towards the end of 2004, a few weeks prior to the first one being published.

Kill and Eat
When I wrote that this conversation belonged somewhere else, I meant it. This was actually overheard by a friend of friend who runs a bar in Spain. This and the mercenary story (page 27) were one conversation between two people he was serving drinks to. It was too good to cut, so I made two stories and four characters out of it, changed the settings, and put myself there to maintain the stylistic continuity of the column.

Museum Judgement
The basement tea shop of the National Portrait Gallery. I never did grow that beard.

Boxes
Service entrance, unknown business, Flitcroft Street, Central London.

Burger Hags
McDonald's, Bethnal Green Road, April 2006.

Clock on a Stick
This is one of my favourite pieces, mainly because of the guy's sheer exasperation, and his description – which he struggled for a moment to come up with – of Big Ben as "a clock on a stick". The fact that his mate was quite dry and knowledgeable made him the perfect counterpoint. They were a remarkable double act, and I consider it my immense good fortune to have waited to cross a road

alongside them when they were on such good form. It happened on a very hot afternoon in summer 2005, directly in front of Camden Underground Station on the high-street side.

Bookmark
There was a strange moment two weeks after this when I was in another pub talking to two people I knew whose Garth Brooks/ Garth Crooks confusion had been the basis of another column (page 125) when Bookman Man appeared again. I asked him if he ever read the newspaper and he said a few people had told him he'd been in it. I confessed to writing it and felt that I should give him some money for his contribution; he'd helped me make some. Sadly, I only I had a couple of pounds on me at the time, and I've not seen him since.

Cat Eater
This place is close to a large psychiatric hospital in Mile End and is popular with the outpatients, which makes it a good venue for unusual dialogue.

Deal or no Deal
The pub where this happened is on Clapham Road in South London and had always been one of those places where people were either watching a horse race or an Old Firm game. The spectacle was all the more unusual for the fact that it happened in autumn 2005, months before Deal or No Deal *became an overground phenomenon. The drinkers had evidently discovered and claimed the show as their own, and were reacting to each result with the same mixture of rapture and disappointment that might ordinarily have followed the scoring of a winning goal.*

Black Country Express

As luck would have it, I was sitting with the editor of the Guardian Guide *on a train from Birmingham to London when this took place. I couldn't have hoped for a stronger demonstration of the column's veracity. It was the middle of August 2005, and the train's air conditioning was broken to the point where people were getting out at the interim stops just to get some fresh air. The "Sad Kerry" in the magazine was the ever-luckless Kerry Katona.*

Bus Labours Lost

Upstairs No. 8 bus, vicinity of Bethnal Green Road. This was quite early in the morning, and I was left wondering – given the nature of their discussion and their disparate origins – how they knew each other and where they were headed together at that time of day.

Unlucky Man

Westbound on the No. 8 bus. As the man was sitting next to me I was worried that he might see me making a note of his conversation, so to avoid suspicion I wrote key phrases down in the grid of the crossword of the newspaper I was carrying and quickly filled it up. At the time I was quite pleased with myself, but when it came to writing it up it proved to be even less decipherable than my usual notes. It's not a technique I've repeated since.

Carpet Scream

The window in question is just across the street from my own, and in the summer months it's a source of near-constant inspiration. The first woman – who lives in the flat – has an unbelievably loud voice and, although I can always hear her, I actually have yet to set eyes on her. Though I have an entire file in which I have recorded her outbursts over the years, I have only used them once, mainly because I'm terrified she might somehow get wind of it and start shouting at me.

Launderette
Calvert Avenue launderette, East London, summer 2006.

Caviar
Sticklers for extreme detail might care to note that this was in Terminal 3. Until the law changed, Caviar House was – apart from Wetherspoons – the only place in the airport where you could smoke and drink at the same time. The nature of the seating forces people together there, which makes it a far better eavesdropping venue than the pub.

Chanel
Christmas 2005, Chanel shop, Sloane Street.

Courier
In a classic "be careful what you wish for" moment, I was in my office wondering what to write when this guy came to the door. He talked for so long, and on various other matters as well, that I was concerned I might forget the best of it, but the fact that I was able to transcribe it as soon as it was over means this is probably one of the most verbatim of them all. I've often wished he'd come back.

Chicken Women
This happened outside the Warrington Hotel in Maida Vale, early September 1995. It was a couple of days after the Notting Hill Carnival, but I got the impression that for these ladies this level of alfresco exuberance was probably a year-round thing.

Oz Dogs
This was in Aubergine *in Chelsea, formerly home to Gordon Ramsay. It was enough to put you off your food. That said, if I had been paying for the meal it would probably have annoyed me a lot more.*

Genius
This was outside the Old Ship Inn in Hammersmith, immediately after I'd emerged from the subway where the tout incident (page 147) happened. The embankment was thick with rock 'n' rollers having a drink before the gig, and it was one of those rare occasions when I was gifted two conversations in the space of five minutes.

EEC
Train from Waterloo to Norbiton, 2006.

But is it Art?
Jeff Wall exhibition, Tate Modern, August 2005.

Crane Train
Railway line outside Gosforth, Glasgow to London train, November 2006.

Garage
This happened in the Texaco garage on Shoreditch High Street in early January 2006. Standing as it does on the boundary between the "fashionable" part of the area and the distinctly more old-fashioned one, this twenty-four-hour facility – which also boasts the area's most consistently functioning cashpoint – is a beacon for eccentric behaviour of all kinds. The staff there have seen their share of action, but this guy really managed to confuse them.

iPods

This was the first All Ears *piece ever published, under the original title of 'Earwigging' in the February 2005 edition of* Good for Nothing. *The actual incident happened in November 2004. I was flying to Sweden to work on an article about deodorants and brand identity, and was aghast – and probably a bit jealous – to find myself sitting in the airport terminal with two women who were off to California to go shopping. iPods weren't as common then, and it was the combination of the sheer modernity of their mission and the details of their private lives that persuaded me to write it down, though I had no idea then what I would do with it. I do however remember feeling quite judgemental about them, especially Woman 1. Given her dislike of physical contact, I told myself, "I bet your record collection's awful too, I bet you don't even need an iPod." I described her as ugly just to complete the effect. What she actually looked like I can't remember. Horrible, really. But then you have to do something while you're waiting for your plane.*

Library

This was in Bethnal Green Library – a fantastic place, one of the few traditional libraries left in central London, and not nearly as debauched as I have made it sound.

Lottery

Newsagents, south end of Charing Cross Road.

Wintour Wired Jaw

Foliage restaurant, Mandarin Oriental Hotel, Knightsbridge, London 2005.

Industrial Action

This was in the Swiss Cottage branch of McDonald's in the middle of the 2006 World Cup. The workmen – who, with the exception of Workman 1, seemed to be mostly Eastern European – were clearly getting accustomed to the more traditional aspects of British labour relations.

Knife Mum

This was on a No. 11 from Liverpool Street to Kings Road, summer 2005, an hour's journey when it's busy, so it would have been unusual to get nothing at all. I can recall the mother's ferocity still, her talk of police "storming" the bus and the kid's air of resignation.

Museum Flirtation Failure

Cafeteria of the Tate Britain, during the Joshua Reynolds exhibition, summer 2005.

Nana Nanoo

The back garden of The Owl & Pussycat, off Shoreditch High Street, summer 2006.

Newt Planner

This was on a train from Waterloo to Southampton. From a writing point of view it was perfect – I could hear him, he couldn't see me, and he really did talk for almost the entire journey. I took so many notes that in the end I chose to leave a lot of the detail out for fear of reprisal.

Crook Brooks

The Golden Heart, Commercial Street, East London, summer 2006.

Oz Debt

This chap was marching about at the south end of Brick Lane on market day. I was using the samosa as a cover, but he definitely realized I was listening to him, hence the look of hostility at the end, I suspect.

Phone Bust

This is actually a distilled version of a conversation I had with a friend of mine whose inability to lie convincingly is matched by a compulsion to try and confuse his girlfriend as to his whereabouts, a state of affairs that leads consistently to social disaster.

Plane Woman

British Airways flight from Cairo to London, June 2006.

Plumber

In my own front room, autumn 2006. The plumber is actually an old friend of mine. We don't see each other very often, but when we do he's a dependable source of anecdotal action and insight.

Swiss Ball

The truth of this is that it was a conversation between two people I was having lunch with in a restaurant. I moved it into a pub just to give the anecdote a bit of distance. It is a true story though, and the descriptions of those involved are accurate.

Public Nuisance

This chap was in the Pride of Spitalfields, which stands on a kind of fault line between the City of London and what's left of the old East End, and entertains a varied clientele to say the least. If you want to hear someone say something noteworthy, you don't have to stand at the bar here for too long.

Shot in the Face
Upstairs on the No. 8, eastbound, November 2006.

Sonic Chameleon
These two were sitting in Hoxton Square. What was interesting about them was the way in which he seemed to typify the East End's latest arrivals – blasé, consciously cosmopolitan and sexually opportunistic – while she (in my mind at least) represented the area's indigenous population – forced to tolerate it all in the interests of commerce.

Touts
This was in the underpass that connects Hammersmith Underground to what used to be known as the Hammersmith Odeon. The occasion was the Iggy and the Stooges reunion tour of August 2006, a memorable evening, made all the more so by this landmark communication failure.

Train Boy
As described, this happened on a Manchester to London train. It's a highlights package of the boy's comments, which went on for most of the journey – but it's accurate inasmuch as most of them did fall in the first fifteen minutes. I was travelling with a friend who sat further down the carriage, and as I told him the story when we arrived, a woman who overheard us then joined in our conversation and started talking about how the experience had made the trip "unbearable". Personally I was quite happy, as I knew I could get a column out of it that would just about offset the price of the ticket.

Lift Yank
Queensway Station, September 2006.

Trouble with the Normal
This happened in The Griffin, Leonard Street, East London – other than public transport probably the most consistent source of material I know of.

Pub Food
Another one from The Griffin, Man 2 was me, which explains how I knew what he was thinking.

God Loves…
Newsagents, Bethnal Green Road.

Paint Points
A restaurant in Soho, summer 2007.

Sneeze
On a train heading south from Edinburgh, December 2006. In the hour that followed, the same woman managed to get into an argument with the guard over her ticket, which she then recounted over the phone to a friend before calling her dad and spending a good ten minutes browbeating him into picking her up from the station.

Tube Mad
Camden Town to Old Street, c.11.45 p.m. Friday night. Never again.

The Water Margin
Business centre, Richmond, 2007.

Scots Wheel
Princes Street, Edinburgh, December 2006.

Bagel Bike
This happened in the southernmost bagel shop on Brick Lane, January 2006. Bike man remains a significant though inscrutable figure in the area to this day.

ACKNOWLEDGEMENTS

Special thanks to Neil Boorman and Tim Lusher, without whom things would never have started, and to Alessandro Gallenzi for ensuring that they got this far. I am much indebted to those people who either submitted conversations directly to me, or had ones with me that I twisted around: Ian Allison, Rowan Chernin, Mark Carter, Dan Davies, Gezz Geddings, Scott King, Paul Ormesher, Tom Stubbs, Jake Walters and David Whitehouse. Thanks to George Babbington for some priceless free advice. Above all, thanks to everyone who was in earshot and said something worth writing down.